Obamanutz:
A Cult Leader Takes the White House

Joy Tiz, MS, JD

OBAMANUTZ: A CULT LEADER TAKES THE WHITE HOUSE

Copyright © 2009 Hero's Prose, LLC
Palm Desert, California 92260

First Printing: August 2009

ISBN-13: 978-1-448-6534-3
ISBN-10: 1-44865-343-6

Library of Congress Cataloging-in-Publication Data

Tiz, Joy, 1955-
   Obamanutz: A Cult Leader Takes the White House / Joy Tiz
   p. cm
   Includes biographical references and index
   ISBN-13: 978-1-448-6534-3
   ISBN-10: 1-44865-343-6
   I. Title

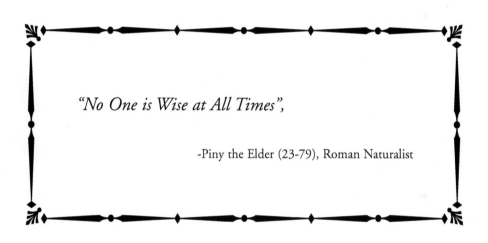

"No One is Wise at All Times",

-Piny the Elder (23-79), Roman Naturalist

Table of Contents

Introduction

America did not elect a new president on November 4th, 2008—America enabled a cult leader to take over the White House. A man with no executive experience, deeply disturbing associations, and gaping holes in his history was elevated to the highest office in the land—not based on merit, but impelled by the force of a mass movement.

Those who are just now awakening to reality need not feel alone. No tyrant rises to power without a lot of help. Barack Obama had an enormous machine of enablers known as the mainstream media, which ultimately became a genuine ministry of propaganda for the campaign and, later, for the Obama presidency. Hitler and other mass movement leaders knew the importance of harnessing the press. Only a small fraction of the media--often referred to as alternative—were willing to examine the actual facts about the mysterious man who wanted to be leader of the free world. Talk radio and independent bloggers became the modern version of Nazi resistors with their chain letters and ham radios.

All of the information we ever needed to understand who Barack Obama really is has always been readily available. Examining the information and talking about it required a level of sophistication and moral courage that is apparently lacking in America these days. Still, there remain deeply troubling questions about Obama and his past that the Mainstream Media continues to ignore.

Experts don't agree on the precise definition of "cult." A definition is really only as good as it is useful, and when we look at the Obama phenomenon cult is a word that fits nicely. Nikita Khrushchev used the term "cult of personality" to explain the dogged persistence with which Stalin's admirers clung to their incongruous notions of Stalin's greatness notwithstanding his barbarity.

If we look at what we know in the light most favorable to Obama—that is, over-looking for the moment his troubling associations with anti-American mentors and mysterious past—and we consider candidate Obama as the media wanted us to see him, it's indisputable that something far beyond a well-orchestrated and moneyed campaign swept America and the world.

Enormous crowds and fainting fans are generally reserved for teenage girls at rock concerts, not political rallies. Articles cropped up everywhere referring to Obama as "the messiah." Photos appeared with lights and halos around Obama. Obama merchandise sells: walk into a major bookstore and run right into the Obama shrine—a table covered with books, photos and all manners of Obama paraphernalia.

And somehow, half of the country managed to overlook how freakish it all was. In the 1930s, there were plenty of wise people who were getting a bit creeped out by Hitler's character and his Mein Kampf. In the months before the 2008 US presidential election, lots of people were getting creeped out by *Dreams from My Father: A Story of Race and Inheritance* and *Audacity of Hope: Thoughts on Reclaiming the American Dream*.

Comparisons of Obama's abrupt rise to power with that of Hitler are in no way meant to trivialize the Holocaust. But elections have consequences, and my Canada Free Press readers are telling me that Obama's positions, in particular his fierce opposition to the protection of infants born alive after botched abortions, open the door for legitimate comparisons. I will let you decide.

Credit for Barack Obama's dizzying rise to power has been given to a mainstream media that tossed out whatever journalistic ethics they had left. But despite their dedication, the press alone could not have gotten Obama into the White House. A mass movement of this magnitude required a confluence of events, the most important of which was a discontented population. The machinery for an Obama type of takeover was fired up long before Obama showed up. In fact, Obama himself is the least important detail of the plan. Much has been made of Obama's soaring oratory and personal charisma. Yet while charisma is a fundamental requirement of a cult leader, Obama does not own a monopoly on personal magnetism and upon reflection; we will see that he brought very little to the table.

In *Obamanutz: A Cult Leader Takes the White House*, we explore all of the variables that allowed a candidate as deeply flawed as Barack Obama to capture the United States presidency. Until now, the focus has been on Barack Obama and his story. This approach overlooks the complex convergence of several political, economic, and social issues that made Obama's election possible, if not inevitable.

We have not yet seen what the results of Obama's policies will be, either foreign or domestic; but within a few weeks in office, he managed to set off an enormously destructive and dangerous course of action within our economy that threatens us on multiple levels. We have already seen significant foreign policy blunders and heard him enunciate troubling ideology.

Will more innocents be slaughtered as a result of the nation allowing itself to be taken over by the Obamanutz cult? Is it too late?

We must come to understand how Barack Obama took the White House. We need to study his campaign and presidency to understand how this utterly unqualified and anti-American man was able to rise so quickly to the most powerful office on earth. We need to fathom how he continues to hold so much sway over his devoted true believers. Shaking off denial is always the first step in recovery.

Battered women who get out of abusive relationships and recover invariably acknowledge in retrospect that there were indeed red flags, but they consciously or semiconsciously chose to ignore them because he was just so "charming." Obamanutz: A Cult Leader Takes the White House examines that charm. At the same time, we take an unblinking look at how we let our country devolve to the extent that electing Barack Obama seemed like a good idea.

Chapter 1

The Essence of Cultism

> *"The group displays excessively zealous and unquestioning commitment to its leader and (whether he is alive or dead) regards his belief system, ideology, and practices as the Truth, as law."*
>
> -Janja Lalich, PhD and Michael D. Langone, PhD

Experts don't agree on what a cult is. There are those who believe we are too quick to label any organized movement outside the mainstream as a cult for fear of demonizing some group, unless of course we are talking about Christianity. Others think we ignore obvious signs of cult behavior at our own peril.

It is a unique time in history when the cult discussion has shifted to the story of the forty-fourth president of the United States of America. Nobody can argue that Barack Obama's meteoric rise to power wasn't breathtaking in its speed. Does that mean Obama is a skilled politician whose team used marketing and technology in new and effective ways? Or is something more sinister at work?

Historically, research regarding cults focused on religion. Within that context, there have always been those who insist that religion is but a cult for the simpleminded. But as cult expert Janja Lalich points out, religion is the wrong paradigm to use in the study of cults; it is a psychological, not a religious phenomenon. (1) Use of the term "cult" is fairly recent, evolving from the proliferation in the 1960s forward of drug-fueled group insanity of which the Jonestown massacre is but one example. Earlier research refers to the phenomenon as a mass movement, an organized devotion centered on a charismatic leader. Hitler and Stalin are examples of what we would call cult leaders today. The New Age movement has ushered in batches of small movements, some with cultish characteristics. Much of it was in response to the turbulence of the 1960s drugs and protests.

The essence of a cult is that it is a group or movement that, to a significant degree, exhibits great or excessive devotion to some person, idea, or thing. (2) Definitions are only as good as they are useful. Throughout the Obama movement, apologists have been quick to complain about the suggestion that Obama's supporters' behavior was becoming cult-like. Yet no politician in American history has received such attention and adoration for so little. Admiration is one thing; newspapers publishing photos of a presidential candidate wearing a halo is quite another.

A cult can be either sharply defined or quite diffuse. The glue that holds the whole thing together is the devotion to the leader via a shared commitment. The cult may uphold some ideology it considers transcendent, but the essence of the cult is not its stated purpose; it is the devotion to the cult leader. (3)

Cults or mass movements have always been with us. We have seen the kind of tragedy that can follow an excessive devotion to a cult leader. In common parlance, we throw around the term "cult of personality" when describing the Obama phenomenon. The phrase was used by former Soviet Union leader Nikita Khrushchev, who set about to reform the country after Stalin's reign of terror.

Khrushchev correctly understood that Stalin's ability to grab and hold on to power while committing unspeakable atrocities was due to his success in establishing himself as the leader of a cult.

In a pop culture of moral relativism, we are not supposed to address the question as to whether Obamamania is a cult or a mass movement. There is enormous variability in terms of the relative damage done by cults. Not all mass movements ultimately evolve into cults. Many remain small and self-contained, like the Heaven's Gate suicide cult. Others, like the Church of Scientology, have an elaborate inner working that is designed to protect itself from excessive scrutiny by not allowing its more bizarre practices to be on public display unless Tom Cruise is promoting a film.

Is there such a thing as a "good" cult? No, because being held sway by a charismatic cult leader mandates the subjugation of individual free will. Thus, it matters not if Obama fanatics engage in some positive activities as part of their Obama devotion; the subjugation of their individual free will is far too damaging. It's helpful to think in terms of a continuum in relation to the degree of influence and control over the followers. (4)

> "The purpose of a cult is to serve the emotional, financial,
> sexual, and power needs of the leader." The single most
> important word here is *power*.

This is the overarching concern with mass movements: irrespective of the stated agenda, the true purpose of the cult is to further the power of the cult leader.

This is why cults are invariably dominated by left wing ideologues. Hitler's Nazi Party was socialist, although liberals to this day insist on embarrassing themselves by calling Hitler a "right winger." Fascism is the exclusive domain of the Left, explained brilliantly by Jonah Goldberg in *Liberal Fascism: The Secret History of the American Left from Mussolini to the Politics of Meaning*.

That is not to say an ill-intentioned power-grabber couldn't identify himself as a conservative, but conservative ideology cannot, by definition, become a cult. The foundation of conservatism is individual liberty, the antithesis of the mass movement. Cultism requires the surrender of free will in service of the cult leader. This is why they often end so badly. Good leaders like Lincoln and Gandhi knew to try to "curb the inherent evil in a mass movement."(5)

Throughout history, at the center of every cult is the charismatic cult leader. In fact, the charismatic leader defines the cult.

According to Lalich, a "charismatic commitment" is required. This is the point at which the believer becomes a true believer, *at the expense of personal freedom.* (6) We saw a lot of that going on at Obama rallies.

The leader's personal charisma becomes the hook; his authority flows from it. The leader sets the stated ideology, and the believers have to adapt their beliefs, thoughts, attitudes, and behaviors to the leader's. (7) In other words, "Yes we can!" The conversion often takes an activist stance according to Lalich. But the ideology is irrelevant; the devotion is to the leader, not the cause. The cause will be taken up based solely on the certitude of the leader. Doctrine need not be understood, but it must be believed in. In fact, the doctrine should be intentionally vague; slogans and special meanings are essential as members get a sense of inclusiveness from their symbols and perceived "secret" messages from the leader. (8)

If this were not the case, one wonders how Germans could have been persuaded to participate in the Final Solution based on ideology alone.

Cult followers are often idealistic, but in no way should we believe they are happy.

If there is one issue upon which non–Obama believers and true believers can agree, it is that Obama has charisma. While elusive and difficult to define, the quality of charisma can be described as a special charm or appeal. One could barely begin to count the number of times we have heard Obama described as "charismatic." Obama's sessions with campaign volunteers have been described as having a "revivalist flavor." (9) We have all witnessed the swooning crowds at campaign events. Even Obama's detractors are quick to acknowledge his "likability." Obama is admired by some for his quality of "coolness," and compared to JFK's elusive detachment. But charisma itself does not a cult leader make. Personal charisma is a useful quality. Being charismatic is only troublesome when combined with psychopathology. Thus, in addition to that elusive likeability quality, the cult leader has to possess a significant degree of some type of psychopathology before he becomes a real menace.

Establishing charismatic authority requires three characteristics according to Zablocki and Robbins in their research on the sociological study of cults: effective oratory skills, ability to create legend or myth, and a capacity for innovation or success. (10) We just never get tired of hearing about Obama's charisma.

Obama's oratory skills have become popular mythos. However, bestselling author and *Wall Street Journal* columnist, Peggy Noonan recently addressed Obama's soaring rhetoric by suggesting that the smitten print out the text of his speeches. Never has so much *nothing* been said so well. Or, more accurately, *read* so well. We now know that Obama can't deliver the most banal communication without benefit of teleprompter.

The entire Obama campaign was based on mythology. His fictionalized life story created a captivating narrative. Millions were beguiled into believing that this man was something exceptional, even talismanic. "The One," however, turned out to be nothing more than a Chicago politician with troubling associations and a cryptic past.

While the Obama presidency will be catastrophic for America, his campaign was a spectacular success. It took colossal skill to convince half of the voting population that Obama was qualified to be leader of the free world. No campaign has ever raised more money than Obama's, and the campaign set new standards for exploiting technology and the media. The phantasm created was that such a spectacular campaign would somehow ensure a spectacular presidency.

There are those who will argue we can't compare the Obama phenomenon with the rise of a murderous dictator like Hitler. To suggest this is to attempt to define a cult backward, that is, by calling a movement a cult based on its ultimate outcome. We don't diagnose a medical condition by waiting to see how it ends. It is the nature of the cult leader, not the final results that define a cult.

How Cults Form

A mass movement or cult can only take off when the right confluence of circumstances makes it possible. The overused phrase "perfect storm" is a perfect fit. A culture is at its most vulnerable when the population is discontented. Historically, tyrants have benefited most in economic crises. No matter how gifted and charismatic the leader may be, he cannot create a mass movement out of nothing. (11) The technique of a mass movement, as Eric Hoffer puts it, is to "inject the society with an ailment and then offer the movement as a cure." (12) Well-functioning societies are not vulnerable to the effects of a charismatic cult leader. When we review the rise of other destructive mass movements, we will see that widespread discontent with the current order was essential to the rise of the cult leader.

Once the conditions are right, the way opens for what Hoffer refers to as the "man of words." These men of words grab the attention of the masses. The words are meant to and can convey a strong sense of urgency because the listener understands that no matter how soaring or inflammatory the rhetoric, there will be no immediate action. (13) "The fierce urgency of now!" This allows the population to experience the emotion of the rhetoric but remain comfortable. The man of words has the power to undermine established institutions.

The quality of the ideology being espoused is a minor matter. It is the skill of the man of words that determines the course of the movement. Although the specific idea being spouted is not of any grand consequence, another essential element of the mass movement is hatred. (14)

A worthy enemy is necessary to fire up the base, and the leader can show his shrewdness by how skillfully he chooses and identifies the enemy. (15) If the society is ripe for one mass movement, it's ripe for another. Putting the movement into action, however, requires a clearly identified object of hatred.

Thus, as Hitler demonized the Jews, so the American Left in 2008 had its intense and unrelenting hatred for George W. Bush. "Common hatred unites the most heterogeneous elements. To share a common hatred, with an enemy even, is to infect him with a feeling of kinship, and thus sap his powers of resistance." (16)

The Making of a Mass Movement

Despite the apparent uniqueness of each well-known mass movement, the truth is, the leaders are remarkable in their lack of specialness. From Stalin to Hitler to Jim Jones and every other cult or mass movement leader, we find remarkable little substance or specialness and far more in common than unique. All mass movements are largely imitative. Even Nazi propaganda was more imitation than original. (17) In fact, mass movements are virtually interchangeable. Landau and Lalich suggest there may be a "Cookie-cutter Messiah School" somewhere; so similar are the traits and pathologies of cult leaders. (18) In reality, it is their psychopathology manifesting that creates the similitude.

For all the hoopla about Obama as "The One," the truth is he is remarkably unremarkable. Other than an above-average ability to read from a teleprompter, there is little outstanding about the man who would become the cult leader in chief.

Obama is a Chicago politician with virtually no experience running anything. We know he went to Ivy League schools, but Herculean efforts have been made to keep his academic records secret, which could lead some suspicious types to conclude that perhaps his grades were less than stellar. We know he was appointed editor of the *Harvard Law Review*, but there is no record of Obama ever actually contributing to the journal himself to show us his legal brilliance.

His track record as a state senator from Illinois is hardly inspiring. The few bills he did sponsor were primarily hijacked from one of his mentors so Obama could stick his name on something. Like many others in the left wing of the Democratic Party, Obama has stuck to the old-school radical party lines with nary an original idea.

For all of the Obama exhortation to show bipartisanship, actual records show Obama as backing some of the worst bipartisan special interest legislation and positively championed corrupt political systemic arrangements. The media uncritically labeled Obama a "reformer" based on his promises to change Washington, cavalierly ignoring the fact that he did no reforming while he was actually in Washington. (19)

Led by Oprah Winfrey, half of the country came to believe that this remarkably unremarkable man was anything from the Second Coming to the Messiah, and the One.

As we review the limited accomplishments and gifts of Obama, we will see that it does not strain the limits of credulity to stipulate at the outset that Obama was not elected president of the United States based on merit.

Let us dispense with the issue of race. According to the mainstream media, America really, really wanted to elect a black president. That may or may not be true. But it's not relevant. Obama's race did not cause a cult to form. If America is so fixated on race that we *had* to elect a black president, there were plenty of qualified black Americans we could have chosen. The 2008 election was only about race for the Left. Obama's ethnicity became one more tool in his arsenal with which to bludgeon the other side. Choosing the leader of the free world based on skin color is more absurd than going to your local car dealer and insisting on buying a blue car with no concern for mileage or mechanical condition. It's preposterous and offensive for the media to tell us we elected Obama based exclusively on his blackness. Or more accurately, *half* blackness.

What we did do is allow the Left, as represented by the mainstream press, to lead us around by the collective nose on the issue of race, elevating a non-issue to the status of the issue on which an entire election had to turn. Justifiable criticism of Obama's policies or worrisome associations was invariably met with strident accusations of racism.

Chapter 2

The Fourth Estate in Ruins

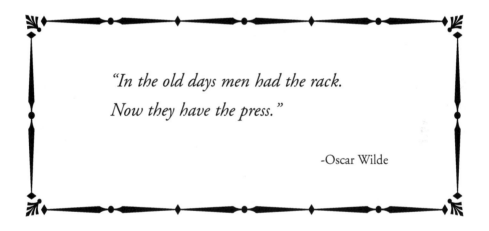

"In the old days men had the rack.
Now they have the press."

-Oscar Wilde

I recently asked a friend, one of the most well-informed people I know, what the original purpose of a free press was. His answer floored me: "to give them a way to express their ideas."

The job of the press is supposed to be to follow politicians around and write down what they say and do. Our Founding Fathers thought the right of the press to perform that specific job was important enough to address it in the very first amendment to our Constitution. Under English common law, wrongful statements against government officials could result in jail or fines. Our founders understood the essential service provided by a free press in protecting a fledgling democracy. If the system was working as it should, politicians and reporters would be natural enemies.

The American mainstream media was hijacked by the Left some time ago, but not until Barack Obama came along did the press become a true ministry of propaganda. No politician has exploited the media to the degree that Obama has.

As former CBS newsman Bernard Goldberg has observed, all news starts at the *New York Times*. It's the *Times* that determines what news gets covered on any given day; the rest of the media just waits for cues from that bastion of balanced reporting. Never in our history has the media been so completely unabashed in pushing its liberal agenda. Goldberg correctly refers to the relationship between the mainstream press and Obama as a "slobbering love affair." (1) It's embarrassing.

Other tyrants, including Hitler, have been able to count on the support of the media to spread their propaganda. Though today's media went a lot farther than openly endorsing Obama's candidacy, which is bad enough by itself. Remember, these people get maximum constitutional protection because they are supposed to be informing the public, not pushing political agendas.

The media also had a responsibility to investigate and report the truth about the man who wanted to be the leader of the free world. There was plenty in Obama's background that demanded deeper inquiry. There was plenty of information about his past and his associations that was easy enough to find. The media made a conscious choice to abdicate what little sense of responsibility they had left; they simply flat out refused to report facts about Obama that ran afoul of their fantasies.

The behavior of the mainstream media during the 2008 election is nothing short of a genuine constitutional crisis. Wrapped in the First Amendment, the press intentionally ignored legitimate news stories, used their power to harass private citizens perceived as a threat to the Obama candidacy, and unashamedly made up facts. The media set about a savage shredding of Republican presidential candidate John McCain's vice presidential pick, Alaska governor Sarah Palin.

Demonstrating just how deep their depravity now runs, the press didn't hesitate to abuse Palin's children when it suited their purpose. They used their connections and influence to attempt to destroy United States citizen Joe the Plumber, whose crime was asking Obama a direct question about tax policy. They made Joe's life a living hell for months to extract their revenge and issue a warning to any other uppity citizen who might consider asking impertinent questions of their candidate.

Chicago Tribune columnist John Kass asks,

> Why is Obama allowed to campaign as a reformer, virtually
> unchallenged by the media, though he's a product of Chicago
> politics and has never condemned the wholesale political
> corruption in his hometown? (2)

None of this is to suggest that there is no place for opinion in journalism. There is a place for editorializing. It's called an "editorial." Journalists are free to express their opinions. What they cannot do is disguise their opinions as facts. The current crop of *New York Times*–led sycophants have no trouble cavalierly making up facts as they go along while hiding or distorting those facts that don't fit their agendas.

During Hitler's reign, young members of the Resistance relied on ham radios and chain letters to communicate with each other. Today's independent conservative bloggers and the alternative media have picked up those noble mantles. Small but mighty, the blogosphere and talk radio became the only reliable news outlets for any truth about Obama that might have put his canonization in jeopardy.

Cable "news" network MSNBC provided favorable coverage of Obama over McCain in September 2008; 73 percent of all the stories on MSNBC about McCain were negative, compared to only 13 percent about Obama. (3) Compare MSNBC to the network decried by the Left as an evil right wing cabal, FOX News: The Project for Excellence in Journalism reported that 40 percent of FOX's McCain stories were negative and 40 percent on Obama were negative. (4) Even hard-core liberal political hack Terry McAuliffe acknowledged FOX's "fair and balanced" campaign coverage.

Americans should be outraged, not only at the obvious pro-Obama bent to the news they were fed every evening, but at the media's total and complete abrogation of its responsibility to report the truth on matters that any thinking American would have found deeply concerning regarding Obama.

Why Wrong Said Rev Matters

Barack Obama's associations should have given the media plenty to work with. He has a long history of association with America-hating radicals. In fact, the more we learn about Obama, the more we have to wonder if this man knows *any* normal people.

Rather than do their actual jobs and investigate these associations, the media instead chose to attack and marginalize anyone who dared raise questions about the judgment and character of the man who would be president. Fox News's Sean Hannity brought up Obama's former pastor, Jeremiah Wright, and was demonized by the Left. Hannity was actually called out by then-senator Obama. Elected officials targeting private citizens for harassment is a dangerous road to travel and an excursion we saw under Hitler and other fascist regimes.

Barack and Michelle Obama spent over twenty years in Jeremiah Wright's church listening to vile hatred toward Jews and whites being spewed. The Obamas exposed their young daughters to Wright's racist rants, along with Wright's tinfoil hat-worthy conspiracy theories. Obama thought highly enough of Wright to have him officiate his and Michelle's wedding and baptize his two little girls. Wright was not an incidental figure in Obama's life. Obama himself admitted to using Wright as a sounding board to make sure he wasn't losing himself in the hoopla. (5)

This, we were told by the mainstream press, was insignificant. After all, Obama said he didn't hear any of that "hate-whitey" stuff. That should be good enough for the rest of us, and if it's not, it's only because we are *racists*.

Wright launched *Trumpet*, the official magazine of the Trinity United Church of Christ (TUCC), in 1982. In 2007, *Trumpet* gave an award to anti-Semite hate spreader, Louis Farrakhan. The Dr. Jeremiah A. Wright Jr. Trumpet Award was given to "epitomize" Farrakhan's greatness. (6)

Wright was lavish in his praise for the Nation of Islam leader: "his integrity and honesty… an unforgettable force, a catalyst for change and a religious leader who is sincere in his faith and his purpose." (7)

And just who is this bit of epitomized greatness, Louis Farrakhan? Farrakhan's rancid rhetoric spans three decades of bigoted and hateful statements targeting Jews, whites, and gays. Farrakhan often refers to Jews as "bloodsuckers." Mr. Greatness Epitomized makes the daffy assertion that Jews controlled the slave trade. Paranoid loon Farrakhan is a never-ending font-of-hate speech directed at Jews and whites, as well as spinning wild yarns about Jewish conspiracies and Jewish collaboration with Hitler, all the while blithely overlooking the fact that American Jews have historically been staunch supporters of civil rights.

But never let the facts get in the way of a good obscene tirade. Screwy Louie is, like Wright, unimpressed with America's status as a superpower. "The real evil in America is not white flesh or black flesh. The real evil in America is white supremacy." (8)

Farrakhan is the leader of the Nation of Islam (NOI), an Afro centric organization founded in 1930. According to discoverthenetworks.org, it was founded on traditional Islamic teachings, augmented by heretical accretions, including the notion that blacks are "Asiatic." In the 1930s, the Nation was pushing for a separate black nation in the United States, entirely segregated from whites in every facet of life. Allegedly, Allah created the black race before all others and that the white race was not created by Allah but by a scientist.

Marxist Malcolm X, one of the higher-profile Nation of Islam leaders, was excommunicated for revealing the sexual hijinks of former leader Elijah Muhammad. Farrakhan, outraged at Malcolm, took over as the new face of the Nation of Islam. Malcolm X was assassinated, an event Farrakhan has tried to justify as recently as 1993.

In the 1970s, a faction named the Death Angels formed, hoping to earn extra Allah points by slaughtering as many white people as possible. The highly successful organization managed to murder seventy-one whites in a spree known at the time as the Zebra Killings. The Nation paid the legal fees for all of the killers but one.

Farrakhan's Nation of Islam group is by far the most recognized of all NOI organizations, based in the Mosque Maryam in Chicago. Farrakhan has set the tone for the group's hostility toward non-blacks, most especially Jews. Farrakhan sees the United States as hopelessly racist and continues to press for complete segregation from white society.

One can easily understand how Wright and Farrakhan hooked up and became such good buddies. The real mystery is: what the hell was Obama doing with these people for twenty-plus years?

Reverend Wright preaches black liberation theology, a virulently radical political ideology that enjoys tax-exempt status by calling it a religion. Trinity's ideology is rooted in the writings of Dr. James Cone, author of *Black Theology and Black Power*, calling for the liberation of black people by *any means necessary*. Cone taught that Christianity as practiced in the United States is the Antichrist and that white theology is not theology at all. (9) Inspired by this nurturing view of Christianity, Obama is so taken with Wright that he memorialized part of one of Wright's revealing sermons:

> It is this world, a world where cruise ships through away more
> food in a day than most residents of Port- au- Prince see in a
> year, where white folks' greed runs a world in need, apartheid
> in one hemisphere, apathy in another hemisphere... That's the
> world on which hope sits! (10)

Obama's confounding decision to join Wright's church is only slightly easier to understand in the context of his political aspirations. As a community organizer, he needed the help of local pastors to gain credibility with the local population. In fact, Obama had a longstanding aversion to Christianity. His mother was an atheist. Obama's grandparents attended churches with radical leanings His father and stepfather were Muslims. There is nothing in Obama's background to suggest an inclination toward any religion. His only religious training seems to be the education in Islam he had during his time in Indonesia with his Muslim stepfather.

> To listen to Wright—more of an apostle of the left than the Christian church—the model for blacks is alienation, deep resentment, separation and grievance. All of which leads to militancy. Militancy is important. It's the sword dangled over the head of society. Either fork over more tax dollars, government services, and patronage or else. And unlike the Reverend Moss and his kindred, I'll specify the "else." Civil unrest. Disruption in cities. Riot in the streets. (11)

Sounds just like what we were looking for in a new president. Let the healing begin!

Had we relied exclusively on the much-vaunted mainstream press, none of us would know who Jeremiah Wright was. The *New York Times* declared the Wright issue a non-story and that, as they say, was that. Legitimate concerns brought up about Obama's association with the rabid hatemonger were met with charges of "guilt by association" and the ubiquitous "racist" assertions. After flip-flopping and mishandling the situation, Obama delivered his race speech, which the toady press hailed as the *most important speech on race ever*, and there was rejoicing throughout the land.

Obama's Other Crazy Church

Long before coming under the spiritual tutelage of Wright, young Barry Obama was finding religion at the First Unitarian Church of Honolulu, sanctuary for military deserters and draft dodgers. Upon his return from Indonesia, the youngster continued his spiritual development at First Unitarian, sanctuary to the Students for a Democratic Society (SDS). Yes, Bill Ayers again. Starting in 1966, University of Hawaii students and professors raised funds to donate directly to our enemies, the Viet Cong. By 1968, the SDS began publishing "The Roach."

First Unitarian provided support and sanctuary to American hating radical extremists as well as draft dodgers and deserters.

a much closer military connection one he has not talked about publicly. Had a reporter asked Obama: "So what *were* you doing during Bill Ayers' fugitive days?' An honest answer would be: "I was going to Sunday school at a church which had provided sanctuary to US military deserters."

While John McCain was being tortured as a prisoner of war in Hanoi, First Unitarian Church of Honolulu at which the elementary-age Obama would later attend Sunday school after returning from Indonesia in 1970 or 71 was sheltering deserters and AWOLs recruited by "flirty fishing" coeds from a Students for a Democratic Society (SDS) group known as "The Resistance." The deserters' exploits were front page news for months on end in mid-1969 Honolulu. They were also proudly trumpeted by the Honolulu SDS tabloid, "The Roach." (12)

Obama thought highly enough of his Hawaii radical church that when his grandmother, Madelyn Dunham died in 2008, her funeral service was held at First Unitarian.

Rashid Khalidi

While plumbing the depths of media depravity, we would be remiss not to give a special shout-out to the *Los Angeles Times*. We can add another radical anti-Semite to Barack Obama's list of very troubling friends: Rashid Khalidi, former spokesman for the original terrorist, Yasser Arafat.

As Stanley Kurtz told radio talk show host Hugh Hewitt;

They [the American people] would be horrified, Hugh. They would be horrified. It would be like saying the strongest advocate for the Palestinians and the greatest critic of Israel in the United States was close to Obama. And you know something? He is, and he was and he is. And so friends of Israel are rightly horrified by this. (13)

Following the traditional career trajectory of washed-out radicals, Khalidi went from terrorist advisor to academia as a professor at the University of Chicago. He eventually would take over the Middle East studies program at Columbia, described as a "bubbling cauldron of anti-Semitism." (14) There is no dispute that Obama and Khalidi have been friends for years. In 2003, Obama attended a party for Khalidi to celebrate his transfer to Columbia. The party was sponsored by the Arab American Action Network (AAAN), which had been founded by Khalidi and his wife. In an amazing coincidence in a long series of amazing coincidences, AAAN just happened to receive money from the Woods Fund, a Leftist organization. On the Woods Fund board: Obama and Ayers. Amazing! The truth is that Khalidi, Ayers, and Obama were practically best friends. (15)

Ayers and his bride, Bernardine Dohrn, attended the Khalidi fete, and Obama had the special honor of heaping praise upon his good friend and America-hating terrorist supporter. All of which was captured on video for all to enjoy. The *LA Times* managed to obtain a copy of the video. Being principled journalists, they immediately buried it.

The *Los Angeles Times* has a video of the Democratic presidential candidate delivering a speech, celebrating a pro-terrorism friend, and the *Times*, in its journalistic wisdom, determines this is not newsworthy? Did the American people have no need to know that the future president parties with terrorists, both foreign and domestic?

The Low-Hanging Fruit

"Losers don't follow the messiah because he is leading them to a promised land but because he is taking them away from their miserable selves." (16)

Misfits are often the first to be attracted to a mass movement; they are the most willing to wreak havoc on the existing order. (17) The radical Left always tries to win over the least productive among us with promises of government freebies. Liberals never tire of inventing new categories of victims, absolving the nonproductive of responsibility for their own circumstances.

As Hoffer has pointed out, contented populations are not easily drawn into a mass movement. Barack Obama's young liberal base was easy pickings.

But how did the rest of the country get sucked into this cult? The demonization of George W. Bush and the unpopular war in Iraq helped to soften the ground for a destructive mass movement. The mainstream press kept an iron grip on the dissemination of information about their candidate. We fell for the man of words who:

- discredits current institutions;

- creates a hunger for faith;

- furnishes the doctrines/slogans; and

- undermines those who are not vulnerable to the mass movement, which are those who are getting along well in the current order. (18)

Obama's entire campaign was an endless populist attack on nearly all of our established institutions. Wall Street was an instrument of Satan. Americans are bitter clingers. Recall those revivalist campaign rallies and the "yes we can" chanting. Yes, we can *what* was never clearly articulated.

To win the election, Obama had a mandate to undermine the successful and well-adjusted among us. While spewing the unoriginal Marxist claptrap about the "middle class," Obama made it clear that if you are financially successful, you only got that way by exploiting the masses. If you are wealthy, someone else must be poor. He promised to finally stick it to those Wall Street fat cats. He built an entire campaign around convincing the population they were miserable, and the only cure for their collective angst was to put Obama in the White House.

The perfect embodiment of the man of words strategy was Peggy the Moocher, the woman who told a reporter that since Obama was going to the White House, she need no longer worry about paying her mortgage or putting gas in her car. Obama would take care of all of that.

Unfortunately, Peggy the Moocher is not an aberration. An alarming number of Americans went to the polls with Peggy the Moocher's mind-set, "All I have to do is elect Obama, and the government will take care of me."

That kind of thinking requires more than just the debonair man of words. It requires the general dumbing down of America.

Some voters pulled the lever for Obama because they genuinely believed all of the campaign gibberish and sloganeering; they joined Peggy the Moocher in formalizing their entitlement demands upon the government. Other, more thoughtful voters listened to Obama on the campaign trail espousing some centrist ideas and concluded that though he may have some radical associations, he would surely govern from the center and not plow the country into complete chaos.

Obama's election is incontrovertible evidence that America has gotten really, really dumb.

Chapter 3

The Great American Dumb Down

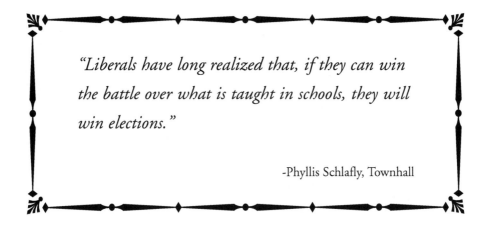

> "*Liberals have long realized that, if they can win the battle over what is taught in schools, they will win elections.*"
>
> -Phyllis Schlafly, Townhall

Appearing at the Conservative Political Action Committee, 2009, former House Speaker Newt Gingrich commented on Barack Obama's first speech to the nation: "How dumb does he think we are?"

How dumb *are* we? Really dumb.

Decades of entrusting the federal government with our children's education has led, inevitably, to the dumbing down of an entire nation. Our public school system has failed to provide the most basic and elementary skills, while at the same time functioning as a ministry of propaganda for left wing causes.

Nobody can seriously argue that our kids are getting smarter. Teachers unions have done yeoman's work tirelessly crusading against accountability. Standardized tests, we are told, are inherently biased against disadvantaged students. Social promotions are essential to safeguard self-esteem.

Ken Blackwell describes the risks inherent in the current fixation over "fairness" that pervades our public school system. He reminds us that standardized testing has been demonized since the 1970s, when activists challenged the Scholastic Aptitude Test (SAT) as biased against women, minorities, and anyone who did not know what a regatta is. Liberal histrionics notwithstanding, the SAT and ACT are constantly being reviewed and refined as new data comes in. Most importantly, the tests can be administered in a way that the testing process is identical for all students. The more standardized the procedure, the less room for examiner bias.

Blackwell warns about a liberal creation known as the Fair Test, a Boston organization dedicated to eliminating standardized testing in education. Although their stated agenda is to "end the misuses and flaws of standardized testing," the organization really considers any and all uses of standardized testing to be "misuse." (1)

And just who is leading the charge for the elimination of standardized testing? According to Blackwell, Fair Test receives funding from the Woods Fund, of which Bill Ayers is a board member. Whenever something destructive is going on in education, all roads eventually lead back to Ayers.

The one issue that liberals refuse to bother themselves about is the fact that the SAT and ACT are excellent predictors of academic performance. As Linda Chavez points out, your ACT or SAT scores will not predict your future success in life, but they are consistently reliable predictors of academic performance. (2)

Under the banner of multiculturalism and diversity, we just keep getting dumber.

The Left, for all of their posturing about helping the poor and minorities, never hesitate to destroy any genuine opportunity for advancement that might diminish their own power or irk the teachers unions.

The Obama administration is making it easier than usual to mine the depths of liberal cruelty. For all of their endless jactitations of compassion for the less fortunate, the current crop of liberals in charge wasted no time setting about to destroy the futures of disadvantaged minority schoolchildren in Washington DC.

Finally finding one government program they could do without, the liberals passed the omnibus spending bill, which included express language, killing the successful Washington DC school vouchers program.

Proposed by former president George Bush in 2003, the DC Opportunity Scholarship (OSP) provides school choice to parents of the most disadvantaged students. Passed into law by Congress in 2004, the program provides up to $7,500 in scholarship funds to approximately 1,700 children who would otherwise be doomed to gang and drug-infested academically deficient public schools run by incompetent union-protected bureaucrats.

The program has been operational long enough now for data to be in showing the effectiveness of the program. Only a liberal would need this explained. The DC taxpayers spend $14,400 per pupil each year to keep them in dangerous and inadequate schools. For half that amount, parents can send their children to schools that are not run by somnambulant bureaucrats and gangbangers. To put it in the language of euphemism so favored by the Left, without vouchers, eighty percent of 1,700 schoolchildren would be forced into public schools that have not made "adequate yearly progress" per the No Child Left Behind Act.

The rate of minority enrollment in the voucher program is approximately 99 percent. The family income hovers around $20,000. The DC public school system spends far more than most districts and has nothing but shame and wrecked lives to show for it. Barely half of all public school students graduate, despite all of the ingenious manipulation by liberals to make us believe those piles of taxpayer dollars are not being jettisoned by union thugs and lazy bureaucrats.

Considering DC's stellar track record of academic excellence, one might expect the effective and cost-efficient OSP would be welcomed. Such confusion is understandable if one insists on focusing on what liberals say they want rather than what they actually accomplish. Without the benefit of a PhD in education, most of us can figure out why the voucher program works. Studies have consistently shown that students perform better academically without bullets whizzing over their heads and when taught by teachers who are smarter than they are.

According to the Heritage Foundation, parental satisfaction is also having a salutary effect on the kids. Parents feel positively about their children's safety in the voucher schools and notice their children take on a more positive attitude toward learning. The voucher program hands some actual parenting power back over to the parents, and the kids are the clear winners.

Virginia Walden Ford spoke at CPAC 2009 about the DC voucher program. In the 1990s, Ford had no choice but to send her son to a decrepit public school. For years, then-mayor Marion Barry and the City Council were ferociously opposed to any type of union-offending school choice. Barry eventually stunned the world by changing his mind, or sobering up, and writing a prochoice article for the *Washington Times*. The message is clear and unambiguous; even Marion Barry can understand this.

Ford's son eventually received a scholarship to Archbishop Carroll High School, where he would thrive. In a happy ending, guaranteed to make liberals apoplectic, Ford's son eventually enrolled in the Marine Corps and served his country valiantly in Iraq.

Hoping to prevent similar disasters in the future, Democrats wasted no time destroying the DC voucher program. Buried in the *national tragedy known as omnibus*, is specific language exterminating the successful school choice program. The odious omnibus includes a whopping $140 billion for the superb Department of Education. The legislation mandated that no federal funds can be used to continue the DC voucher program beyond 2010 without approval of Congress and the DC City Council.

In other words, our current Oval Office resident just sentenced 1,700 children to dangerous and ineffective inner-city schools.

Obama and Congress did this, well aware of the cost-effectiveness of the voucher program—the positive effects on the children and their parents, as well as the manifest long-term benefit to the community. But we needn't bother ourselves with that if we are liberals. As long as we make the right noises about our compassion and concern for minorities, we're cool. Everyone knows the real racists are those conservatives who refuse to understand the importance of preserving a thoroughly dysfunctional status quo.

Representative John Ensign (R-NV) audaciously tried to insert language into Omnibull in hopes of saving the DC voucher program. It failed fifty-eight to thirty-nine.

Is anyone wondering if one of those fifty-eight sends their kids to DC public schools? Dick Durbin (D-IL) provided this well-reasoned argument against vouchers: the program would take money away from the public school system.

That is a lot like taking matches away from arsonists.

Durbin doesn't think we should "give up" on the DC public school system. Most thinking people are perfectly happy to "give up" a dangerous and ineffective plan. But liberals never trouble themselves with facts. We are to judge strictly on their stated, phony agendas. As long as they say they are all about helping the disadvantaged, we are to take them at the word.

You don't have to dig very far below the surface to see that liberals, for all of their claims to be the sole arbiters on all matters of compassion in the world, are, in fact, extraordinarily cruel. Nary a day goes by when we don't hear some celebutard like Sean Penn waxing downright lyrical over some murderous thug of a dictator, be it Hugo Chavez or Fidel Castro. Our current president staked out the ever-popular pro-infanticide position, startling even Barbara Boxer. In the Left's most recent display of endless love and compassion for the downtrodden, they choked the life out of a creative, effective, and uplifting school choice program, thus dooming innocent children to sadder if not shorter lives in gang-infested hellholes.

According to Representative Ensign's Web site, during the 2006–2007 school years, more than 6,500 crimes were committed in DC public schools.

Forty-five percent of senators send their children to private schools, almost four times the rate of the general population.

Half of all teenagers in DC public schools are in schools with enough crime incidents to be classified as "persistently dangerous."

The Dangers of Diversity

Not content to merely throw away billions of your hard-earned tax dollars on substandard schools that refuse to teach the most basic academic skills, the Left has also hijacked your children's social development. Under the rubric of teaching "diversity" (which may be the most dangerous word in the English language), public schools have become indoctrination centers, dedicated to teaching impressionable young people that America really ought to be ashamed of itself.

The 2008 National Education Association's (NEA) annual convention was a veritable anti-America carnival; provocative anti-marriage, anti-Christian, and pro-gay slogans were everywhere. Resolutions were passed that had nothing at all to do with education; only social issues were considered worthy of discussion. Members didn't feel the need to bother themselves with such trifles as math or science, or heaven forbid, history. Public education now concerns itself strictly with the pressing issues of the day: bashing George W. Bush, gun control, and global warming. (3)

The gay lobby has become very pervasive and heavily involved in drafting curriculum. The pressure is on for schools to hire gay teachers as role models and teach children about sexual orientation; ideally, the program will expand to reach preschoolers. (4)

The fine educators of NEA believe your children should have direct access to sexual information and condoms without your involvement. And your government happily grants the public schools the authority and resources with which to inculcate a wildly liberal agenda to your kids. Not surprisingly, the mere suggestion of school choice is met with extreme turbulence.

The term "diversity" is liberal code that has nothing to do with the stated agenda of "multiculturalism," which is supposed to be the study of different cultures. Diversity, as defined by liberal academics, means pushing extreme left wing values onto innocent schoolchildren with impunity. (5)

Borrowing from Saul Alinsky, the academia thugs are quick to marginalize any parent who dares to question the soundness of their curriculum. A concerned parent will be met with extreme derision while being told, "No parent has ever complained about *that* before!"

In other words, you are a crazy, racist, right- wing homophobe. It is worth noting that Islamofascists use exactly the same tactic; any criticism of Islamic violence is met with howls of "Islamophobia!" The goal is to convince you that *you* are the one thinking irrationally.

Kevin Roberts of the Catholic Family Caucus, speaking at CPAC 2009, cautioned that public schools are over feminizing our young men. He is echoing what Rush Limbaugh has called the Oprafication of our culture. Roberts points out that this feminization of males is ultimately going to make our country less safe as fewer young men pursue military careers and other positions in which male authority is a clear advantage, if not a mandate.

The hijacking of our schools has been going on for decades; we are now experiencing the repercussions. John Dewey, in addition to inventing an incomprehensible system for hiding library books, has long been considered something of a pioneer in modern education. Dewey believed the purpose of school was not to educate but to socialize the child. Dewey eschewed notions of an objective truth and authoritarianism. By the 1970s, it was quite fashionable to encourage kids to reject their parents' values. (6)

Majoring in Sedition Studies

The early 1980s ushered in a new era in psychology even further moved from reality. The theory of "humanism" in psychology liberated us from outdated notions of morality and Christianity. We were told not to pass judgment on behavior. A child's behavior could not be "wrong" or "right;" it could only be "inappropriate" or "appropriate." A competing theory, B. F. Skinner's behavioral psychology, taught that human behavior can be explained in terms of stimulus, response, and reinforcement, not unlike lab rats pressing bars for cheese. Liberal professors embraced the absence of morality in both theories. Use of Skinner's behavioral model provided boundless opportunities to shape behavior without the knowledge of the subject, reducing humans to mere organisms easily manipulated and controlled.

About this time, the burned-out radicals of the 1960s were finally getting out of school, only to return to ensconce themselves in the make-believe world of academia. This is where Bill Ayers resurfaces yet again. He is far from a minor figure in "education." Among the left wing radicals who run our schools, Ayers is a demigod. As recently as 2008, Ayers was elected Vice President for curriculum of the American Education Research Association, the largest national organization of education professors and researchers. (7) Thus, it would appear that he has not exactly been shunned by his peers following the revelations about his violent past. If your kids' minds are being poisoned with abhorrence for America and anti-Semitism, you can be confident Ayers's tentacles have reached your school.

> There's something about a good bomb… night after night, day
> after day, each majestic scene I witnessed was so terrible and
> unexpected that no city would ever again stand innocently
> fixed in my mind. (8)

So said Ayers, yet another of Barack Obama's miscreant friends. Despite the campaign's ludicrous talking points about Obama being a mere child of eight when Ayers was planting bombs, there is no question that the relationship between Ayers and Obama is of long standing. Stanley Kurtz has researched the Ayers-Obama connection and found that the unrepentant domestic terrorist's tentacles run far and deep. According to Kurtz, Obama and Ayers have a "genuine political connection." (9)

Bill Ayers is the spoiled-brat son of Thomas Ayers, former CEO of Commonwealth Edison and trustee of the Tribune Company, as well as former chairman of the board of Northwestern University. Thus, his son with minimal gifts, had easy access to academia. Ayers grew up in the affluent Illinois suburb of Glen Ellyn and attended Lake Forest Academy and the University of Michigan. (10)

Ayers admits to a great fascination with explosives. If not for his father's wealth and connections, one has to wonder if young Bill, whose conduct disorder was never properly diagnosed, would have gotten away with so much havoc.

To escape the torment of being born to wealth and privilege, Ayers joined the Students for a Democratic Society (SDS), a radical group looking for an excuse to destroy things. The unpopular war in Vietnam served the radicals well, as did the civil rights movement.

In 1970, Ayers joined the Weathermen, a radical group that helped LSD guru Timothy Leary break out of prison and stockpiled dynamite, which the supposedly brilliant Ayers stored at his apartment. Predictably, some of the dynamite exploded, killing Ayers's then-girlfriend. (11)

When all was said and done, Ayers and the Weathermen were credited with thirty bombings aimed at destroying the defense and security infrastructure of the United States (12). Ayers would later joke about escaping prison on a technicality. One wonders what all the fuss over the Obama-and-Ayers friendship was about.

Super patriot Ayers boasts about his accomplishments: participating in the 1970 bombing of New York Police Department headquarters, bombing the Capitol building in 1971, and bombing the Pentagon in 1972. Ayers would write, "We'd already bombed the Capitol, and we'd cased the White House. The Pentagon was leg two of the trifecta." (13)

Terrorist Ayers would have done considerably more damage had he not been so incompetent. In his 2001 book, *Fugitive Days: A Memoir*, Ayers writes that he is not "ruling out entirely" using violence in the future. On September 11, 2001, Ayers told *The New York Times* that he didn't regret setting the bombs; he felt they hadn't done enough.

From 1995 to 1999, Ayers led an educational foundation called the Chicago Annenberg Challenge (CAC). Ayers remained on the board until 2001. In 1995, Barack Obama, with zero executive experience, was brought on board to dole out over $100 million dollars to various left wing organizations. The stated agenda of the CAC was to "improve Chicago public schools." Not surprisingly, with Ayers and Obama at the helm, CAC's own in-house evaluations show no evidence of educational improvement following CAC's intervention. (14)

Ayers co-chaired the "collaborative" that shaped educational policy. Any suggestion that Ayers and Obama had just a passing acquaintance is preposterous.

CAC's educational "reform" program was meant to substitute radical activism for academics. As Stanley Kurtz describes it, "The CAC's agenda followed from Mr. Ayers' educational philosophy, which called for infusing students and their parents with a radical commitment, and which downplayed academic achievement tests in favor of activism." (15) As David Horowitz points out, the Ayers method is alive and well today in our colleges and universities offering course credit for activism.

Kurtz also raises the question of how Barack Obama, right out of law school with no executive experience, managed to land a position at the top of a new foundation. Despite the campaign's protestations to the contrary, no one would have been appointed CAC chairman without the approval of Ayers. In addition to the six documented board meetings Ayers and Obama attended together, there would have had to have been at least a half dozen more, and Kurtz believes it is "highly likely" that it goes way beyond that. The pair served on a number of small committees charged with hammering out bylaws that created the foundation, which would have to involve a "fair amount" of contact.

Funding from Annenberg went to a variety of left wing organizations, a veritable "alphabet soup" of groups, most of which share ideology with Reverend Jeremiah Wright. (16)

Stanley Kurtz raises yet another question: why is it that Barack Obama never mentions the only actual experience he ever had—his time at Annenberg?

It gets worse when the kids get to college. According to David Horowitz, the University of California at Santa Cruz offers courses in community organizing, teaching students how to put together a revolution. Lest you think it's just another nutty California thing, Horowitz points out that the University of Texas offers a course on murderous thug Che Guevara (17). A member of the Communist Party USA has taken over the women's studies department at the University of California.

Ayers is a leading advocate of social justice teaching. Even young evangelicals— that is, the children of the religious Right—have been deluded into believing in "social justice;" eighteen- to twenty-nine-year-old evangelicals voted for Obama, in spite of his record on abortion. Many of these young people claimed that it was the pursuit of social justice that put them in the Obama camp. "Social justice" is just more aged hippie jargon; it has no real meaning other than to disrupt the current social order. So effective was this inculcation that thirty-two percent of eighteen- to twenty-nine-year-old evangelicals voted for Obama, twice the number who voted for John Kerry in 2004. David Horowitz defines "social justice" as shorthand for opposition to the American traditions of individual justice and free markets. So pervasive is the Ayers social justice model that teachers weave radical ideology into core subjects; for example, using an Iraq body count to teach math (18). Students have no frame of reference to see how absurd this is. Schools today emphasize America's past mistakes and injustices, rather than her achievements.

The goal of teaching social justice is to convince students that they are victims of an unjust, oppressive and racist America. "A few years of this kind of 'education,'" and the kids are primed for a takeover by community organizers who will mobilize them to vote for the Far Left. The plan is working. In 2008, seven out of every ten voters between eighteen and twenty-nine favored expanding the role of the government and believe that the government should be doing more to solve our problems (19).

Future teachers are fully indoctrinated into radical Leftist ideology. Teaching materials are provided by special interest groups with distinctly left-wing agendas. School districts invite these groups to conduct "professional development" training, at taxpayer expense.

Phyllis Schlafly sums it up: "When a teacher engages in this type of advocacy in lieu of teaching literature, math, history, or science, the teacher is engaging in political indoctrination." (20).

Bill Ayers's textbooks are currently in use at 1,500 schools; they are among the most widely used of all texts. Ayers is opposed to achievement tests in favor of activism. The US Department of Education lists fifteen high schools that have adopted mission statements declaring that their curricula center on "social justice."(21).

Columbia, the alma mater of Obama and Ayers, has become a madrassa by way of its Middle Eastern studies department. As is the case with numerous similar departments in other universities, the Middle Eastern studies department is an anti-Israel, a pro-Hamas, and a Hezbollah propaganda arm.

David Horowitz told Sean Hannity on the Sean Hannity show March 9, 2009, that the current goal of public education is not to provide students with academic knowledge; it is to organize an anti-capitalist revolt.

Chapter 4

The Putrefied Pop Culture's Pick

At the same time William Ayers was hijacking our schoolchildren, the popular culture was decomposing. With the advent of the Great Society and the disintegration of the nuclear family, the decline of our pop culture parallels the disintegration of our educational system. Radicals grabbed control over both.

Before MTV debuted in 1981, music had personal associations. A certain song would evoke a memory or a feeling personal to the listener. Then MTV came along and told us what images we were supposed to associate with the music, thereby effectively killing a large part of our collective imagination. But MTV's biggest contribution to the collapse of decent society has to be the introduction of reality TV. Exploiting as many mentally disturbed wretches they could find, MTV lowered the bar in entertainment, effectively turning the vulgar into the mainstream. Reality TV has contributed mightily to the ruination of pop culture and the abandonment of common decency. Celebudoc Drew Pinsky says that reality TV participants are actually more narcissistic than most professional entertainers. Observing the extreme narcissism we see in Hollywood, this is quite a statement.

MTV rolled out its first reality show in 1992. *The Real World* assembled seven young people together in a SoHo loft, filming them twenty-four seven. As expected, there was plenty of chaos and acting out. Dr. Pinsky's complaint about this type of show is that it lacked any type of "balancing commentary." (1) In other words, the vulnerable young MTV audience was bombarded with images of unhealthy behavior with no adult in the room to explain any of it.

By 2000, reality TV had exploded. As Pinsky points out, these shows reward contestants for "ruthlessness, exploitation, authoritarianism, self-sufficiency, and vanity" (2); in other words, narcissistic traits are heavily reinforced.

The danger, according to Pinsky, is what he calls the "mirror effect"—that is, by viewing provocative or shocking behavior enough to the point it becomes "normalized, expected or tolerated"—becomes increasingly reflected in our own behavior (3). To put it another way, repeated exposure to dysfunctional behavior leads viewers, the most vulnerable of whom are adolescents, to believe such behavior is normal; and the susceptible viewer ultimately begins to mimic the destructive behavior.

Little wonder, then, Pinsky reports that the level of narcissism in America is at an all-time high (4). Barack Obama's narcissism has been tolerated because our pop culture has made narcissism seem normal. Young Americans watching addled misfits like Paris Hilton and her ilk now seek fame for its own sake, a prize they hold in higher regard than doing anything useful with their lives.

The Internet is a lot like the automobile. A wonderful tool that improved life in dramatic ways, we can't imagine life without our cars. Autos also kill, maim, and injure tens of thousands of people every year. The Internet is as horrible as it is useful; rampant porn, social networking sites, and chat rooms are like cesspools. Kids who spend too much time playing games online are turning into zombies. It's not the Internet's fault; too few parents care enough to monitor their kids' online activities.

The Internet has proven to be fertile ground for narcissists to act out. The Internet allows users to create an online identity, which may bear no resemblance to reality. Creating a new persona is a classic coping mechanism for narcissists (5). The very act of creating a false self creates a feeling of self-importance. Thus, social networking sites are incubators for narcissistic traits (6).

For previous generations, the question: "Where were you when Kennedy was shot" has served as a conversation starter as well as a catalyst for exploration of a shared history. It would seem that the quintessential question will soon be: "Where were you when you found out Michael Jackson was dead?"

For the record, I was at the gym. Credulous, I trusted that the Jackson story would get a few minutes of coverage before Bret Baier retuned. My jejune confidence that Charles Krauthammer would momentarily be providing commentary about actual news was hastily crushed. Abstrusely, Fox News brought Shepard Smith in to cover this astounding turn of events.

You know what would be really shocking? Michael Jackson dying at the age of 87. That would have been a real stunner, well deserving of the nauseating non-stop narration that should be reserved for heads of state.

Time really stands still on the treadmill when you are listening to a fervid Geraldo lamenting Anna Nicole Jackson's "shocking" death.

All other news of the day having been declared inconsequential, Fox proceeded to indulge in unnecessary and disproportionate keening about the calamitous death of the world's most famous pedophile. The same Michael Jackson who once told a reporter it was "sweet" and "charming" to sleep with little boys and ply them with "Jesus Juice" (known to lucid people as "wine") is has been deified. Jackson, who dangled one of his babies off of a hotel balcony, also obtained those children via a bizarre and labyrinthine arrangement, named one of them Blanket and made them wear burkas.

Jackson is exceedingly popular in the United Kingdom, confirming Mark Steyn's reflection that the United Kingdom is further along than the United States in the march toward complete social and economic collapse. But not to worry, we quit until we're Number One.

Michael Jackson recently converted to Islam (7). Michael's brother, Jermaine, converted to Islam in 1989 (8). Even Religion of Peace failed to deliver true bliss.

Americans know far more about Michael Jackson than they do the history of Iran and its relationship to the United States. Most of what America knows is wrong, having been subjected to pertinacious propaganda in Ayers' based public education.

Which is why the interest in the life and death of Neda Agah-Soltan was so facilely dwarfed by the opulent freak show that surrounds Michael Jackson.

Neda was the beautiful young Iranian woman who was gunned down in the streets of Tehran for the crime of showing up. She showed up to take a stand for freedom and took a bullet in the neck for her aspirations. A relative in the United States had cautioned Neda not to attend any demonstrations, telling her, "They're killing people." To which the lionhearted and prescient Neda replied, "Don't worry, it's just one bullet and it's over" (9).

For just a flicker in time, Neda became an icon, a symbol of the young Iranians' longing for the most elemental liberties. It was easy for Americans to be incensed at the barbarous slaughter of a young woman so lovely and earnest. Young Iran has caught a glimpse of freedom, the inescapable byproduct of advancing technology. The noteworthiness of Neda is in no small measure due to the ease with which young Americans can appreciate her as not so unlike themselves.

Obama's Government to Fix Broken Souls

At what point did Americans discover that their souls were broken and the government is the elixir? A most cursory review of the universal failure of government intervention makes the government an unlikely provenance for a cure for a paper cut, let alone something as grave as broken souls. The notion is daft on its face, yet Michelle Obama campaigned for her husband on the Broken Soul platform.

On the surface, this sort of falderal can be passed over as a campaign stratagem leveled at the more credulous New Agers in the audience who resolutely believe in the capacity of the United States government to dispense spiritual overhauls.

Michelle Obama nimbly pointed out that soul saving would not be yet another government bailout:

"Barack Obama will require you to work. He is going to demand that you shed your cynicism. That you put down your divisions. That you come out of your isolation. That you move out of your comfort zone. That you push yourselves to be better. And that you engage. Barack will never allow you to go back to your lives as usual, uninvolved, uninformed." (10)

It would seem the only candidate adroit at soul renovation rejects the truly soul sustaining ideals of liberty and free will. If anyone should be standing up and demanding their absolute right to be uninformed, it would surely be the Obama supporters.

It requires the audacity of a cult leader to campaign on a pledge of soul retrieving Shamanism.

Barack Obama got a lot of mileage on a manifesto of government intrusiveness and forced unity.

The Metro Sexual Candidate

Throughout the campaign, Barack Obama was idolized for his dapper appearance. Commentators called him debonair and liked the cut of his jib. Indisputably, the man wears an expensive suit well. Europeans loved him; Obama had accomplished the seemingly impossible: he made European men seem manly by comparison.

Despite the contemporary allure of androgyny (how else can we explain Johnny Depp), Americans still like Real Men. In fact, the more Dick Cheney talks, the better we like him. We cheered for Captain "Sulley" Sullenberger who saved the lives of passengers and crew by landing a disabled jet on the Hudson River.

We couldn't get enough of the humble and courageous Captain Richard Phillips who was held hostage by Somali thugs while the Wuss in Chief wobbled. All sane Americans were proud when our magnificent Navy SEALS were finally unleashed to do what they do as only they can.

Ann Coulter unravels it: liberals have canonized single moms, disregarding how badly their kids keep turning out. Sit-com fathers have become dispensable buffoons. Multiple sperm donors per household is becoming chronic.

Unintentionally proving Coulter's point, IVillage.com offers up some advice for single moms raising boys. Presumably, it was not meant to be satire when Andrea Engber assured single mothers that their boys can grow up to be emotionally healthy men, citing a few examples, including Tom Cruise and Bill Clinton! Engber goes on to offer more sapient advice: "Be a little creative in helping your child learn guy stuff. For instance, many single mothers report concern over their son's using the potty while sitting, or playing with their makeup." (11)

It is irrefutable that single moms have the manifest advantage when it comes to teaching their sons how to apply guy liner correctly. How many Oprahfied little boys will grow up to join the military? We've got a future national security crisis.

It's not unusual for boys raised by single moms to become narcissists (see Clinton, William J). The metro sexual male is defined by narcissistic traits, most notably, an over-concern for his appearance that we don't see in Real Men. Sure, they will dress up when the occasion demands, but not without some obligatory grumbling. Liberals didn't learn from Clinton's wussified approach to Islamic terrorism that putting a narcissistic pantywaist in the White House doesn't make terrorists love us after all. Clinton sat on his hands while terrorists attacked us repeatedly: Mogadishu, the USS Cole bombing, the attacks on our embassies in Kenya and Tanzania, please forgive me if I overlooked any others. There was his indefensible refusal to capture bin Laden when the terror leader was offered up to him. Clinton hobbled our military when there were clear opportunities to take the savage barbarian out before 9/11.

A radicalized educational system combined with a decaying popular culture were essential elements in getting a candidate like Obama into the White House.

Chapter 5

Intractable Ignorance

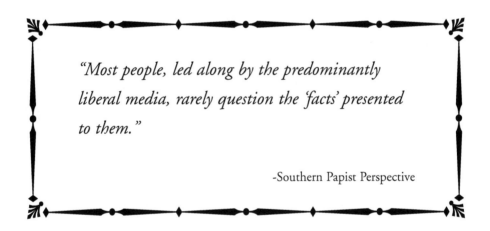

> *"Most people, led along by the predominantly liberal media, rarely question the 'facts' presented to them."*
>
> -Southern Papist Perspective

Barack Obama lied to us throughout the campaign and continues to do so as president. How did over half of the country not notice? The simple answer is that we are just not very good at recognizing when someone is lying to us. Our deception detection skills are inadequate.

Dr. Anna Salter's research on sexual predators gives us some clues as to why we are so often unable to spot a liar. Although her work is focused on deviants, her findings about deception detection are easily generalized to generic liars. The bad news is most liars are not caught because someone recognized their dishonesty. Liars are more likely to be outed by tripping themselves up because their stories keep changing. (1)

> An astonishing number of times, that information is simply ignored or overlooked if the liar is personable enough or glib enough. (2)

Salter also cautions that we are more likely to be fooled if we have a stake in believing the liar. Like, say, he's the hope and change messiah. Many Americans and the media have a lot invested in Obama emotionally. The most savvy among us will also be the most reluctant to admit they were duped; it could be a long wait for the elites in media and DC to acknowledge they fell for the Obama hoax.

Psychopathic liars, according to Salter, are especially difficult to read. They actually enjoy lying, it's a bit like sport to them; thus, they will not display signs of anxiety or distress when they lie. A psychopath lies for the sheer joy of it, even when there is nothing to gain. In the mind of a psychopath, successfully telling a whopper is something akin to scoring a touchdown, and if the listener is already predisposed to believing the liar, half of his work is already done.

Some of Salter's most interesting work is her study of emotional leakage. Understand that there are no reliable behavioral cues of deception. However, if the emotional content of the lie is sufficiently high, there is the risk of emotional leakage. That is, the emotion associated with the words unconsciously leaks out.

Emotional leakage in facial expressions is not reliable; we are looking for micro expressions, that is, the true emotion registers on the face for just a microsecond before it registers consciously. Salter cautions that emotional expressions, which follow words, are likely to be fake. If the emotion is genuine, the feeling registers first, and the words follow.

Right before the 2008 election, presidential candidate Barack Obama made a remark about his opponent, John McCain. As he made the remark, Obama scratched his face with his middle finger. Rush Limbaugh and others were quick to ask if Obama was giving the finger to Senator McCain.

Dr. Salter describes "emblems" as "gestures that are self-explanatory within a given culture and do not require words for interpretation." If the gesture is made consciously, say, for example, flashing the peace sign, there is no deception.

If there is deception, the gesture will be unconscious. Thus, the gesture may be only part of a complete gesture. *The middle finger is one of the emblems that commonly leaks out.*

Much has been made of Obama's speaking skills, or more correctly, teleprompter reading skills. Reliance on the teleprompter makes sense for someone who is deficient in veracity: repeating words, stumbling, and pauses can all be signs that the story line is not flowing naturally because it has not been adequately rehearsed. (3)

Salter gives us a few other insights into how a liar uses words. Note the similarities to Obama's communication style: (4)

- Liars more often evade than outright deny, according to research by Wendell Rudacille.

- Watch for unfinished business: "That's pretty much it," "That's about it," or "That's all I can remember."

- Answering a question with a question.

- Indignance: "Don't be ridiculous!"

- Commenting on the question such as, "That's a hard question."

- Projection: "Someone would have to be sick to do that."

- Accusation: "Are you accusing me?"

- Qualifiers: "I can't say," "I could say," or "I would say." The speaker is trying to take distance from the words. Also language such as "My answer is…"

It's important to pay attention to the actual words, not the perceived implications. Disharmony is a general signal of deception. When people tell the truth, the hands, body language, and voice pitch will all be in harmony (5). The multitudes, even after numerous falsehoods have been exposed, continue to extrapolate what they want to hear from Obama, rather than scrutinize his actual words.

Chapter 6

Barry Soetoro: Profiles in Chaos

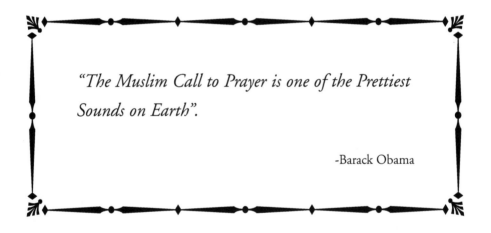

"The Muslim Call to Prayer is one of the Prettiest Sounds on Earth".

-Barack Obama

"It was in this context that I came across the picture in *Life* magazine of the black man who had tried to peel off his skin... I know that seeing that article was violent for me, an ambush attack."

Barack Obama describes his racial awakening at age nine and the impact of the disturbing image of a black man driven to self-mutilation to escape his blackness (Michael Jackson was just a kid at the time). Powerful images.

Also entirely false. *Life* never published any such photos.

Later, Obama would talk about his great struggle with racial issues at Punahou School in Hawaii. Former classmates don't dispute that there were racial discussions at the elite Punahou. But according to Sharon Churcher of the *UK Daily Mail Online*, Barry Obama was not a part of those discussions (1). Hawaii, however, is unique as races have long been mixed on the island. Racial issues in Hawaii have not been the concern of school aged children. Obama's assertions about racial struggles in Hawaii are false.

The character in Obama's alleged autobiography known as Ray—in real life Keith Kakugawa—also disputes Obama's self-portrayal as an "angry black man." According to Churcher, the two had lots of long, "soulful" discussions, but never about race. What Keith does remember was Obama's intense longing for his parents. School friends recall Obama as a "spoiled high achiever" according to Churcher.

Traditionally, works of fiction are identified as such. In his preface to the 2004 edition of *Dreams from My Father: A Story of Race and Inheritance*, Obama admits he cannot honestly say that the voice in the book is not his, or that he would tell the story much differently today than he did ten years ago. (2)

Chicago Tribune reporters Kirsten Scharnberg and Kim Barker interviewed more than forty of Obama's former classmates, teachers, friends, and neighbors and came to the startling conclusion that "several of his oft-recited stories may not have happened the way he has recounted them." (3)

While the mainstream media loves to rhapsodize about Obama's remarkable journey, what deserves more attention is the psychology of the man who is now the most powerful person in the world. Actually, it would have been more useful had the mainstream press been willing to give some serious thought to Obama's mental health before November 4, 2008.

The press is thoroughly enchanted with the Obama biracial, multicultural extravaganza of a life story; so it is no surprise that the actual facts are far from the romantic fairy tale the media has confabulated. Instead, when we examine Obama's childhood and adolescence, we find abandonment, chaos, alcoholism, and abuse, along with an excruciating quest for identity that has not been resolved.

The chaos started long before Obama was born. His maternal grandfather was so disappointed at the birth of a daughter rather than the son he longed for that he actually named the baby girl after himself. One can only imagine what elementary school was like for a little girl named Stanley, who eventually became known by her middle name, Ann. What is the effect on a child knowing you were a disappointment to your father right out of the womb?

Stanley Dunham's own mother committed suicide. Obama describes his maternal grandfather as having a "complete inability to discipline his appetites." (4)

Conspicuously absent from Barack Obama's two autobiographies is the story of his paternal grandfather, Hussein Onyango Obama. Yet Hussein Obama may wield a greater influence on his grandson than the younger Obama acknowledges. In particular, Obama's graceless treatment of British Prime Minister Gordon Brown may be traceable back to his grandfather.

Yet again, it seems that Obama is acting out his pathology at our expense. His appalling treatment of Brown could be written off as another example of this administration's incompetence. But it also looks as if Obama also has his own ax to grind with the Brits and lacks the emotional maturity to deal with it like a grown-up.

Phase one of Operation Ally Alienation was the belligerent act of rejecting Downing Street's offer to allow the new president to keep the bust of Winston Churchill that had been given to former president Bush after 9/11 in a gesture of solidarity and support.

After snubbing the prime minister of America's staunchest ally by canceling a joint news conference in the Rose Garden, the Obamas took their boorishness to the next level during the traditional world leader gift exchange.

Prime Minister Brown presented the new Oval Office occupant with gifts reflecting considerable forethought. Brown gave Obama a penholder made of oak timber from the HMS *Gannet*, a Royal Navy ship that served on antislavery missions off of Africa.

The prime minister also gave ingrate Obama the framed commissioning paper for the HMS *Resolute*, another Royal Navy ship. The ship had been rescued from icebergs by the United States and was offered as a symbol of the goodwill between our two nations. Rounding out the collection of treasures was the first edition of Martin Gilbert's seven-volume biography of Winston Churchill, another symbolic gift representing the alliance of the United States and Britain during WWII.

Not to be outdone, our president presented the prime minister of our most important ally with a collection of his top twenty-five favorite DVDs. In attestation to Gordon Brown's graciousness, the prime minister did actually sit down to view the DVDs, only to discover they are unusable in the UK due to the format.

Mrs. Brown presented the first daughters with lovely outfits from Topshop, a British clothing chain. Michelle Obama gave Mrs. Brown's boys toy helicopters modeled after Marine One, no doubt picked up by an aide at the last minute in the White House gift shop.

Evidently, the president who swore he would change the way the world looks at America is not a fan of the British.

Hussein Onyango Obama had worked as a cook for a British army officer when he became involved with the Kenyan independence movement. He was arrested in 1949 as a sympathizer for the Kikuyu Central Association, the organization that ultimately spawned the Mau Mau. There is no question that the Kenyan penal system of that era was a violent place—mere imprisonment was not considered sufficiently punitive; torture was ubiquitous. Grandpa Hussein's wife tells of the horrific torture of her husband at the hands of the Brits. Some of her recollections are questionable, however: one scene of hell on earth she describes is actually a pretty good description of the process of delousing.

There is also no question that if Hussein Obama was arrested for subversive activities, he was up to something more than just being a good community organizer. He certainly would have been subject to some enhanced interrogation.

The Left wants to paint the Mau Mau as yet another misunderstood group of oppressed victims. The truth is, the Mau Maus were vicious guerilla fighters. Contrary to popular folklore, the Mau Mau slaughtered far more Kikuyu citizens than the whites they were supposedly rebelling against.

Mau Mau membership required taking an oath, which was not exactly frat boy material. The colonial secretary, Oliver Lyttelton, wrote,

> The Mau Mau oath is the most bestial, filthy and nauseating incantation which perverted minds can ever have brewed. I have never felt the forces of evil to be so near and as strong as in Mau Mau. As I wrote memoranda or instruction, I would suddenly see a shadow fall across the page-the horned shadow of the Devil himself. (5)

Little information is available as to the specific language of individual oaths, but we know that the process was taken seriously and had more elements of magic than politics. Kikuyu were under tremendous pressure to take the oath and join the movement.

Counterinsurgency expert Major Frank Kitson describes a Mau Mau body-snatching raid:

> The gang, frenzied by the thought of blood, slashed around with their simis (a Kikuyu sword) and fired their guns. One old man, slower than the rest, was caught and hamstrung. He fell at the feet of his pursuers, covering his face with his arms to protect it from the slicing swords, but a mouse in a mechanical mincing machine would have had a better chance of survival. One terrorist hacked off a foot, and another sliced off his testicles to use later in an Oathing ceremony. A third gouged out his eyes with a staple and put them in his pocket for the same purpose. When they had finished, most of the gang came by to cut and stab the twitching corpse. They then

licked the blood off their simis and moved off into the night,
having first set fire to all the huts they could see. (6)

Other writers claim the oath was far more innocuous. However, a 322-page report by career Colonial administrator Frank D. Cornfield supports the seamier version:

> By compelling Mau Mau members to violate not only Christian
> ethics but every tribal one as well, Mau Mau leaders deliberately
> reduced their victims to a state where a man who took the Mau
> Mau oath was cut off "from all hope, outside Mau Mau, in this
> world or the next." Cornfield found that to achieve this absolute
> loyalty to the movement, "leadership forced its recruits,
> voluntary or involuntary, to seal their oaths by digging up
> corpses and eating their putrefied flesh, copulating with sheep,
> dogs or adolescent girls, and by drinking the famed "Kaberichia
> cocktail"—a mixture of semen and menstrual blood. (7)

Sounds like an earnest group of freedom fighters, right? Again, corroborating that Barack Obama has never known a normal person, his grandfather's support for the Mau Mau was sufficient to get himself arrested. The struggle for independence from the Brits may have been a noble one, but not justification for the kind of depravity indulged in by the Mau Mau. Longtime nationalist leader and Mau Mau manager Jomo Kenyatta studied economics in Moscow in 1932. We are not supposed to make too much of that. The Mau Mau is another example of the power of a mass movement, or cult.

Barack Obama has a grudge against the Brits for their abuse of his grandfather, a subversive who supported a bunch of ferocious guerillas. And as always with Obama, rather than deal with his own inner demons, he uses his position of power to act out. Another campaign promise kept: Obama is most assuredly changing the world's view of America. Perhaps Obama is saving up all the really cool gifts for Ahmedinejad.

Ann Dunham married Obama's father, the focus of his "autobiography." According to Churcher, Barack Senior was not exactly father of the year, and abandoned the family before the child was two years old. He is described as a "drunk and a bigot," who was a cruel man, prone to drunken rages, and an abusive bigamist and womanizer. *Time* reporter Amanda Ripley says Ann filed for divorce in 1964, citing "grievous mental suffering" as the grounds. That may have been the standard grounds for divorce in those days (8). But Barack Senior's third wife, Ruth, claimed he beat her brutally in drunken rages. Obama blames "racism" on both sides for the demise of his parents' marriage.

Most of us will admit to doing less-than-sensible things when we were young and in love. But young Ann Dunham took it a bit farther than sending a few really dopey Hallmark cards. Ann met Indonesian Lolo Soetoro and married him when Barack Obama was about six years old. Starting a new life with a new husband is one thing, but dragging a young child to a third world country is quite another.

Jakarta, Indonesia, in the 1960s was a harsh place for a child. Not much of an infrastructure and staggering inflation, which was creating shortages. Indonesia was a violent place in the era, following hostilities with the Dutch. Not exactly the white picket fences in the burbs. In fact, at the time, Indonesia was a hotbed of anti-colonial rage.

In 1965, communists tried to seize control of Indonesia. One army general understood the threat and was able to rally his fellow officers to prevent a coup. Then-president Sukarno granted the general the power to take "all measures considered necessary to guarantee security, calm and stability of the government." Within the year, General Suharto was the president of Indonesia. Suharto was resolutely anticommunist and protected Indonesia from the fates that eventually befell Vietnam and Cambodia. Suharto provided stability to the nation, as well as economic growth. However, the communist threat was held off at a high price, including a violent anticommunist purge. Suharto was also thoroughly corrupt, and although he protected the country from the very real threat of a communist takeover, there is little question that the nation would have seen more economic growth under a less corrupt regime. (9)

"Barack Obama Sr. was an African colonial to the core; in his case, the apple did not fall far from the tree. All of the telltale signs of Obama's African colonialist attitudes are on full display in the book -- from his feigned antipathy towards Europeans to his view of African tribal associations as distracting elements that get in the way of "progress." (On p. 308 of *Dreams From My Father*, Obama says that African tribes should be viewed as an "ancient loyalties.") The African Colonial sees his constituents not as individuals blessed with individual liberties but rather a flock of sheep in need of being led, oftentimes to their own slaughter. The African Colonial seeks to destroy all forms of democracy. (10)

Barack Obama, however, does not give Suharto credit for his unbroken commitment to fight communism. Rather, he refers to Suharto's regime as "brutally repressive" and blames the United States for supporting Suharto's regime. Obama does not bother himself to ponder what life would have been like for the people of Indonesia had Suharto not been willing to fend off the communist coup. Has the world seen a communist regime that was kind and nurturing? Obama actually saw the democratization of Indonesia as a negative, refusing to accept that democracy can lead to prosperity. In *Dreams*, Obama writes, "Indonesia survived, at least on the surface, financial meltdown and democratization." (11)

Life was hard for little Barry Soetoro in Indonesia. According to Sharnberg and Barker, he was "teased mercilessly" by the other kids. Obama now claims he became fluent in Indonesian within six months, but his teacher recalls it differently and claims he "struggled greatly," according to Sharnberg and Barker. His mother would later say that had she known what had transpired in Indonesia in the years before they moved there, she would never have taken her son there. (12) It seems odd that a woman as politically astute and intelligent as Ann Dunham was entirely unaware of living conditions in the country to which she was bringing her little boy.

Ann eventually left Lolo Soetoro, and Obama went to live with his grandparents when he was ten. After that he would see his mother only sporadically as she pursued her own interests. The Dunhams were the closest thing to a stable family young Barry would have. The only reliable breadwinner in the family, Madeline Dunham, managed to work her way from secretary to bank vice president, which was quite an achievement in her day. Her hard work and discipline enabled her husband Stanley to devote himself to being a slacker. It has been said that Stanley was fond of telling tall tales himself.

When children experience overwhelming trauma, they protect themselves as best they can with a variety of defense mechanisms. There is no question that life for little Barry was traumatic, full of chaos and abandonment, as well as genuine fear. The adults in his life betrayed him and taught him hate and mistrust. Otto Kernberg, in his research on narcissism, states that it evolves as a defense against a cold and unsympathetic parent. The child withdraws part of himself from the unavailable parent and turns it back toward himself, creating a grandiose sense of self. Healthy emotional development was just not possible in young Barry's environment. In Toxic Parents, Dr. Susan Forward describes the "Golden Child," who compensates for feelings of inadequacy by seeking external awards and accolades rather than his own inner confidence. Golden Children are commonly found in alcoholic families.

The Smartest President Ever!

Nary a day went by in 2008 in which we were not reminded that in Barack Obama, we had the chance to redeem ourselves and finally elect a smart president, not like that dopey George W. Bush with his manifest lack of artistry with a teleprompter.

Obama, we were incessantly assured, is a genius. America, we were told, had an exigent need for a brilliant scholar with an Ivy League education. Candidate Obama was at once articulate *and* former editor of *Harvard Law Review*! One could hardly be expected to find a more able leader of the free world.

Bewilderingly, when given the chance to proffer affirmation of his cerebral superiority, Obama declined to liberate his school records. His rival, John McCain was a conspicuous hooligan in college. Obama certainly never has been one to miss an occasion to proclaim his ascendancy, real or imagined.

Yet, colossal efforts have been made to conceal Obama's school records along with the enigmatic birth certificate.

The president has elucidated little about his days at Occidental or Columbia other than to affirm his affection for radical, anti-American Marxists. Obama and his fellow travelers studied the writings of Frantz Fanon, another anti-white, anti-colonialist. Fanon's book, *The Wretched of the Earth*, argues for an entirely new world order by way of "absolute violence." Violence, according to Fanon, purifies. Obama mentor Edward Said was also a Fan of Fanon.

It takes a bit of narcissism to wake up in the morning and think, "Hey, I really ought to be leader of the free world." Coming to such a conclusion in the fourth grade is, to say the least, ambitious. Having some narcissistic traits does not a narcissist make. However, according to the *Encyclopedia of Mental Disorders*, grandiosity is the most important single trait in narcissism.

Could they mean something along the lines of creating the "Office of the President-Elect" and grand speeches in Germany—Obama's messianic image of himself? This is disturbingly common among cult leaders.

Narcissists are also thin-skinned and unable to tolerate any form of criticism. Obama has been quick to lash out at private citizens, including Sean Hannity and Rush Limbaugh; and his administration makes no secret of their wish to shut down Talk Radio, the one reliable outlet for criticism of the government.

Obama's grandiosity is striking. It's in his body language and posturing. It's in his derisive comments about "bitter clingers." In office, Obama has demonstrated early on his sense of entitlement and his belief that he is above the law.

Narcissists can be dangerous. They lack the capacity for empathy. Bill Clinton is a narcissist who learned to mimic normal emotions and convince people he felt their pain. In the words of Peggy Noonan, Clinton is a "great actor." A narcissist needs a constant source of narcissistic supply. They need the constant attention and accolades. Cutting off the narcissistic supply feels life threatening to the narcissist. Many wife abusers are narcissists who fly into rages when they perceive a threat that would cut off their supply. This is why so many women are abused and killed when they make the decision to end the relationship.

Obama suffered through a traumatic childhood. He didn't get the stable, nurturing, loving parents he needed. But lots of people overcome childhood trauma and live healthy, happy lives. What we need to be concerned about is Obama's lack of insight into his own issues. In *Dreams*, he falls into the typical pattern of idealizing his absent parents rather than confronting the reality of who they were and how they treated him. At no point does Obama acknowledge that his childhood caused him any problems; instead, he projects his rage onto white people. Every bad break, including his parents' divorce, was caused by "racism."

This is not a man in touch with external reality. The rage is certainly justified; he was gypped out of a normal, stable childhood. We can all feel angry and sad for what little Barry endured. But we cannot ignore how much Obama has distorted reality. He could have called *Dreams from My Father* a work of fiction. But that would suggest that he knew it was fiction.

The truth about No Drama Obama is that his early life was perpetual drama, which had to have done plenty of damage. What is most disturbing is his failure to deal with it. People do recover from early trauma and abuse, but only if they acknowledge it and allow themselves to experience the feelings that they had to block when they were too little to manage them. Eventually, the experiences have to be integrated into the adult personality; and not infrequently, abuse survivors benefit from professional support.

The current leader of the free world is not in touch with reality. The toady press gleefully accepts his fabrications and denials. And mental health professionals have shown a remarkable lack of curiosity about the mental health of the president of the United States.

Chapter 7

Dreams From My Father, Pathology From My Mother

"Indonesian blacksmithing is spiritually powerful and sacred, and an area exclusive to men. The story is that blacksmiths forged human souls for the next generation"

-Alice Dewey, University of Hawaii

"Like many educated intellectuals in postcolonial Africa, Barack Hussein Obama, Sr. was enraged at the transformation of his native land by its colonial conqueror. But instead of embracing the traditional values of his own tribal cultural past, he embraced an imported Western ideology, Marxism. I call such frustrated and angry modern Africans who embrace various foreign 'isms', instead of looking homeward for repair of societies that are broken, African Colonials. They are Africans who serve foreign ideas." (1)

West African writer, L.E. Ikenga explains that Barack Obama's platitudes about race in America were useless in understanding who he is. Throughout the president's much-adored book, *Dreams from My Father*, Obama claims his identity as African even as he exploits the historical struggles of blacks in America to suit his own purposes.

Ikenga postulates that Obama is an old school African Colonial who is well on his way to turning the United States into a third rate nation. Africa is poorly understood by Americans and this ignorance has served Obama well as he continues to deceive the country.

"The African Colonial (AC) is a person who by means or their birth or lineage has a direct connection with Africa." The AC's worldview has been shaped by European imperialism, rather than the indigenous beliefs of a specific tribe. The AC has little true appreciation for his original culture and traditions, and rather uses them the way one might use a piece of costume jewelry. (2) The African Colonial abhors Western culture yet craves the trappings of wealth and prestige. Obama, in his quasi memoir carried the "blame whitey" theme throughout the text which is the typical platform for the African Colonial Politician.

Barack Hussein Obama, Senior carried the African Colonial's rage and resentment toward colonial conquerors whom he perceived as destroying his homeland. This anger drives the African Colonial to embrace leftist ideologies as a mechanism for seizing power. Barack Junior has set about the well-worn road most traveled by despots by attacking America's traditions such as his "bitter clinger" rant. Obama has assaulted Americans with the largest transfer of private wealth in the nation's history and is hell bent on confiscating as many privately held resources as he can. Obama and his followers over value his Ivy League education in hopes of fooling the masses into thinking they really do know best. And, as Ikenga's African Colonial politician invariably does, Obama lies regularly to the American people about the fictional progress being made to repair the economy.

In the land of the Obamanutz, questioning the African Colonial in Chief is evidence of the doubter's racism and ignorance. Barack Hussein Obama used *Dreams* to stake out and claim his African heritage. His antipathy for our European allies is flagrant.

Barack Senior's early abandonment of his son calls into question just how much imprinting he could have done in shaping Barack Junior's African Colonial ethos. For all of the pandemonium propagated by the *Dreams From My Father* fable, the story of Obama's father is a diversion contrived to further camouflage his identity. Obama's ersatz narratives empowered him to inveigle multiple voting groups. For all of the advertising about Obama being a post racial candidate, he is preoccupied with race and manipulates racial sensibilities to gain advantage. It would be more truthful to characterize Barack Obama as the post-American president.

Obama's mother, Stanley Ann Dunham was not the Dorothy in Kansas heartland girl he fabricated during his campaign. Notwithstanding Obama's dreamy concoctions about the mythology surrounding his father, the predominant influences on him came from his mother and grandparents who were the authors of much of his Anti-American resentment.

Though Ann Dunham was indeed from Kansas, the family relocated to Seattle in 1955. They then moved out to Mercer Island specifically so Ann could attend Mercer Island High School, which earned notoriety when the chairman of the Mercer Island school board, John Stenhouse, testified before the House Un-American Activities Subcommittee, acknowledging that he had been a member of the Communist Party. (3)

When checking out a new school district, normal families infrequently rank "led by communist" at the top of their must haves list. Unlike other parents, the Dunhams did not demand Stenhouse's resignation.

As with Obama himself, his mother's generation of these pseudo-intellectual leftist high schoolers found a way to think of themselves as superior. How? By surrounding themselves with co-thinkers. The *Seattle Times* continues:

"One respite was found in a wing of Mercer Island High called 'anarchy alley.' Jim Wichterman taught a wide-open philosophy course that included Karl Marx. Next door, Val Foubert taught a rigorous dose of literature, including Margaret Mead's writings on homosexuality." (4)

Ann Dunham's parents were at ease with communism. Recall their affiliations with conspicuous communists, Paul Robeson and Frank Marshall Davis. Despite Barack Obama's efforts to minimize his grandparents' religious beliefs, the family did indeed attend church. The Dunhams worshiped at "The Little Red Church on the Hill;" East Shore Unitarian Church. The church's own website boasts of well publicized debates and forums that earned it the Red appellation.

Ann Dunham graduated in 1960 and the family moved to Hawaii.

"Honolulu had just two years earlier been shaken by the Honolulu Seven Trial of Longshoremen's Union leaders and other Communist Party members ending with convictions overturned by a 1958 Supreme Court decision. But just as with John Stenhouse and Mercer Island, this didn't scare the Dunhams it attracted them. Upon arriving in Honolulu, they became fast friends with Davis who had been a columnist for the ILWU's communist-line *Honolulu Record* newspaper. Davis had at one point chaired the Honolulu Seven defense committee. Davis' editor had been one of the Honolulu Seven defendants Koji Ariyoshi. The largest shareholder in the Record was Ed Rohrbough. Ariyoshi's memoir "From Kona to Yenan" describes how he and Rohrbough worked as US military intelligence officers hand in hand with Mao Zedong in Yenan, China during World War II. During and after the war they helped steer US policy toward the Red Chinese and against the Nationalists." (5)

The Communist Party, always on the prowl for a group to exploit, openly promoted inter racial relationships among its members as early as the 1930's. Former classmates of Ann Dunham recall her as having no use for "crew cut white boys". Dunham met Barack Senior in a Russian language class at the University of Hawaii.

In *Dreams*, Obama describes his mother's sentimentalized sensibilities toward black Americans: "Every black man was Thurgood Marshall or Sidney Poitier; every black woman Fannie Lou Hammer or Lena Horne. To be black was to be the beneficiary of a great inheritance, a special destiny, glorious burdens that only we were strong enough to bear." (6)

Obama never needed his father's coaching to learn to loathe America. His mother had little approbation for American traditions and values. Dunham may have been altogether earnest in her belief that socialism was the best apparatus to help the impoverished Third Worlders with whom she so identified. Dunham seems to have been imbued with the theory of the noble savage; the belief that man in his primitive state was free and good. Man was corrupted, therefore, by the accumulation of private property, leading to inevitable inequitable outcomes. The noble savage myth presupposes that civilization is the cause of corruption. Note the consistency of this line of thinking with Ikenga's writings about the African Colonial.

In the puerile fantasy world concocted by Dunham, the Third World was where all of the good people were. When she migrated to Jakarta with her son, she promptly interjected herself into the local Javanese community. She was enchanted by the Javanese culture and rejected her second husband, Lolo Soetoro, when his career with Mobile Oil began to advance. She refused to attend social gatherings with his co-workers, insisting that they were not her people.

Dunham's absorption in Third World folkways eclipsed her enthusiasm for bringing up her young son. She chose instead to pursue a degree in archeology. Alice Dewey of the University of Hawaii recalls Dunham as a craftsman and weaver in Java herself. Dunham considered Indonesia her home, returning to Hawaii occasionally to study and to earn money. (7)

All of this Javanizing meant that little Barry was left with Grandpa Stanley to be treated to visits with the fetid Frank Marshall Davis at a time when normal little American boys were busy with Little League rather than making up pornographic limericks to entertain the "adults."

Dunham became established in Indonesia. She completed requirements for her MA in 1974 although it was not formally granted until 1986. Meanwhile, she was offered a position at the Ford Foundation. (8)

Initially started by Edsel Ford and two executives in 1936, the Ford Foundation has swung far left over the years. Its current objectives include:

> "The weakening of homeland security and anti-terrorism
> measures on the theory that they constitute unacceptable
> assaults on civil liberties; the dissolution of American borders;
> the promotion of mass, unchecked immigration to the United
> States; the redistribution of wealth; the blaming of America for
> virtually every conceivable international dispute; the depiction
> of Israel as an oppressor state that routinely victimizes its
> Palestinian minority; the weakening of American military
> capabilities; a devotion to the principle of preferences based on
> race, ethnicity, gender, and a host of other demographic
> attributes; the condemnation of the U.S. as a racist, sexist nation
> that discriminates against minorities and women; the
> characterization of America as an unrepentant polluter whose
> industrial pursuits cause immense harm to the natural
> environment; the portrayal of the U.S. as a violator of human
> rights both at home and abroad; the depiction of America as an
> aggressively militaristic nation; and support for taxpayer-funded
> abortion-on-demand as an inalienable right for all women." (9)

In yet one more in an interminable chain of coincidences, Dunham ended up working for Peter Geithner at the Ford Foundation, developing the Foundation's microfinance programs in Indonesia. Peter Geithner is the father of current Treasury Secretary and tax cheat. Timothy Geithner also spent his impressionable years outside of the United States.

Obama's mother wouldn't complete her doctoral dissertation until 1992, just a few years before her death. Her final work was the 1,067 page tome, *Peasant Blacksmithing in Indonesia: Surviving and Thriving Against All Odds.*

Blacksmithing in Indonesia is the exclusive province of males. How remarkable fervent feminist Ann Dunham would bestow so much time and effort to the study of a male dominated craft. According to Dewey, blacksmithing Indonesia style is something more than bending metal:

"It's powerful, spiritually powerful. The smithy area is sacred; women couldn't go into that area. The story is that blacksmiths forged human souls for the next generation. There's a carving in one of the temples depicting one of the demi-god heroes as a blacksmith. It's highly symbolic. You put offerings on the anvil. So you have a sacred craft that developed over some 2000 years." (10)

In other words, the blacksmithing vocation which so fascinated Barack Obama's mother is infused in magic and superstition.

Chapter 8

The Narcissist in Chief

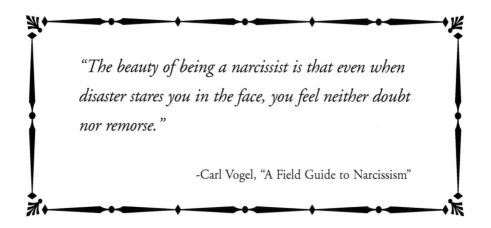

"The beauty of being a narcissist is that even when disaster stares you in the face, you feel neither doubt nor remorse."

-Carl Vogel, "A Field Guide to Narcissism"

In 2008, America elected her first celebrity president. So pronounced was Barack Obama's status as a pop culture celebrity that former rival John McCain ran ads comparing Obama to Paris Hilton and Britney Spears, two pop icons famous for their fame rather than their accomplishments. A quick review of then-senator Obama's record suggests he was coasting in on something other than his meager accomplishments as a legislator and Chicago POL.

A less qualified presidential candidate would have been hard to find. Yet Obama was not only a serious candidate and ultimate victor, but during his campaign, he pranced around, acting as if he already was president and the election was merely a ceremony to formalize his taking of the crown. Obama, albeit briefly, displayed his own seal, which looked remarkably like the president's official seal. He appeared before huge crowds in Europe, acting in front of all the world like a head of state. He argued with General David Patraeus, the general who brilliantly orchestrated the successful troop surge in Iraq. Once Obama finally deigned to meet with the general, he not only refused to acknowledge the success of the surge, the junior senator from Illinois chastised General Patreaus, telling him that while he could understand the statesmen's point of view, he alone knew best when it came to managing the war in Iraq.

Incredibly, there are Obamanutz among us who honestly don't realize that Obama is a narcissist of the worst kind. Most people mistakenly believe narcissism is something akin to egomania or an unusually high sense of self-esteem. The truth is the reverse. Narcissists suffer from self-loathing, not too much self-love.

Narcissism is a personality disorder, meaning a cluster of traits that endure over time and, literally, are part of the individual's personality. These traits go to the very core of the person's identity; they are not transient or situational. The term "narcissism" is being mentioned in the media quite a lot recently, not only due in no small part to the election of Obama, but also because many experts believe that our culture, particularly young people, is becoming increasingly narcissistic.

The most significant feature of narcissism is grandiosity. (1) The narcissist also demonstrates high levels of authority, entitlement, exhibitionism, self-sufficiency, superiority, and vanity. (2) It is important to understand that we all have narcissistic traits; the quality of self sufficiency, for example, can be highly adaptive. We all need a degree of self-reliance. It's more useful to consider narcissism and its elements as a continuum rather than a yes-or-no matter.

Obama is not America's first rock star president; that honor goes to Bill Clinton (also a narcissist, by the way), the first president of the MTV era. Clinton was our first baby boomer president. "Obama, on the other hand is the product of another constituency; one who has no memory of the sacrifices and hardships endured by the Greatest Generation; one for whom a rock star in office is worthy of the supreme adjective: "cool." (3)

Boomers were the first generation to be raised on TV; the next generation was raised on satellite, cable, Internet, video games, cell phones, and other omnipresent technology. "If TV was the babysitter of the Boomers, it became mother, father, teacher, and preacher to all who came after." (4)

The young voters who fawned over Obama have no recollection of a world war, or of the devastation of a Great Depression. Hardship to the Obama generation means not getting the newest version of Xbox or PlayStation. What difference did it make to them if their candidate was superficially glib and profoundly unqualified to hold the highest office in the land? A media creation, Obama fit their image of what a rock star president should be.

It's not in the nation's best interest to put a narcissist in the White House. Clinton's debauchery demonstrated his willingness to put his need for narcissistic supply ahead of the well-being of the country he was hired to serve. Clinton's narcissism was manifestly less extreme than Obama's.

For all of the narcissist's grandiosity, he is driven by a relentless need to pursue and maintain a source of narcissistic supply. Clinton was driven by polls; he made major policy decisions based on poll data. His sexual acting out is also typical of narcissists.

The Diagnostic and Statistical Manual of Mental Disorders (DSM IV-TR) is the diagnostic manual used by mental health professionals. A diagnosis of narcissism requires five out of nine characteristics. Note these traits must endure overtime and must not be reactions to a particular situation or environmental stressor:

1. Grandiose sense of self-importance.
2. Preoccupation with fantasies of unlimited success, power, beauty, or ideal love.
3. Sense of specialness, belief he can only be understood by or should associate only with other special or high-status individuals or institutions.
4. Need for excessive admiration.

5. Heightened sense of entitlement, leading to unreasonable expectations that others should treat him especially favorably or comply automatically with his expectations.

6. Tendency to be interpersonally exploitive. A person with NPD does not hesitate in taking advantage of others to meet his own ends.

7. Lack of empathy, an inability or unwillingness to recognize or identify with the feelings or needs of others.

8. An envy of other people, or conversely, a belief that other people envy him.

9. A tendency toward arrogant behavior or attitude. (5)

In his essay on Obama's narcissism, Sam Vaknin references Obama's haughty body language and condescending attitude. Vaknin also points out Obama's "emotion free language." (6) Commentators frequently describe Obama as cool and aloof.

Some narcissists learn to mimic normal human emotions. Clinton is the master of this; he claimed to feel our pain, and plenty of Americans believed him. Clinton learned how to win people over with his pseudo empathy. Obama has yet to demonstrate anything we could call true empathy; irrespective of the words he uses, there is no real emotional content.

His cavernous lack of empathy becomes more obvious as his presidency rolls on. It could hardly be called empathic behavior when Obama decided to drop all charges against Cole bomber Abd al-Rahim al-Nashiri before Obama's scheduled meeting with the families of the Cole victims.

Obama's plan to reduce tax deductions for charitable donations is not an idea born out of compassion for his fellow Americans.

President Obama's scheme to reduce medical coverage to wounded veterans was dropped after appropriate public outrage. But the question remains: what kind of man even proposes such a thing? The amount of revenue saved by such a measure would be minuscule while this president has no compunctions about spending staggering sums on worthless programs. One has to consider what is in the soul of a human being who would deprive our wounded heroes of their medical benefits.

Millionaire Obama seems not in the least concerned about his own half brother, George Obama, who lives in a shack in Kenya. George's neighbor, Emelda Neigi, has commented, "I would like Obama to visit his brother to see how he is living and improve his way of life." (7)

In *Dreams from My Father*, Obama writes glowingly of his grandmother, Madeline Dunham, to whom he refers as "tut." Indeed, Mrs. Dunham was a surrogate mother to young Barry, stepping up when her daughter took flight to pursue her own interests. Grandma Dunham was the glue that kept the family together and remarkable in her own right, starting out as a bank secretary and working her way up to vice president in an era when it was difficult for women to achieve such success. Yet when it became politically expedient to chastise her for being a "typical white person," Obama never flinched.

More troubling is that despite the success of her grandson, Mrs. Dunham spent her final years in the same tiny apartment in which she reared young Barry. News footage showing Obama outside of his grandmother's home shows a rundown slum of a neighborhood. How could a loving grandson allow the grandmother who sacrificed so much to provide for him allow the woman to live in a ghetto? He surely had the means to provide her with more suitable housing.

As a presidential candidate, Obama often pitched his nationalized health care plans by using his mother's fatal illness. Ann Dunham was diagnosed in 1994 with deadly ovarian cancer. Her son likes to talk about how dreadful it was for his sick mother to have to spend her last days fighting with her insurance company. One has to wonder why her wunderkind son, the brilliant lawyer and future senator, could not have stepped in and dealt with the insurance company on her behalf?

Demonstrating yet again his endless capacity for insensitivity to others, Obama let his mother read a draft of his memoir before her death. That must have been a high point for Dunham, since her son chose to write the nearly entire book about his absent, drunken, bigamist father.

In *Dreams*, Obama writes, "I talked to Jews who'd lost parents in the Holocaust and brothers in suicide bombings. I heard Palestinians talk of the indignity of checkpoints and reminisce about the land they had lost." (8) This is an astounding passage. Is Obama saying that losing land you consider yours or being stopped at a checkpoint is the equivalent of the slaughter of one's family members by Nazis or suicide bombers?

Such is the nature of the narcissist.

The narcissist is also comfortable with dishonesty. Obama regularly looks America in the eye and tells whoppers. Entire Web sites have sprouted for the sole mission of keeping track of Obama's lies. He does it fluidly, with not a trace of shame or anxiety. He is a gifted liar. Documenting all of Obama's lies would require a book of its own. And they just keep coming. His quasi-autobiography, *Dreams from My Father*, is a cornucopia of lies, half-truths, and distortions. "At the end of the day, Barack wants the story to help his political cause so perhaps he couldn't afford to be too honest." (9)

He surely can't afford to be too honest about his deep enmeshment in the cesspool of Chicago politics or his seventeen-year relationship with convicted swindler Tony Rezko. Syrian-born Rezko was a major fundraiser for Chicago Democrats and a good friend of Obama. Obama himself told the *Chicago Tribune* that it was his close personal relationship with Rezko that convinced him their shady land deal was legitimate.

Rezko bilked the Chicago taxpayers out of a fortune, obtaining grants to develop low-income housing projects. Obama did his part by sponsoring bills mandating affordable housing that use funds from renewal bonds. The young Illinois senator also wrote letters for Rezko to make sure the development contracts went to his construction company. Unfortunately, the busy entrepreneur couldn't be bothered to actually provide livable affordable housing units. His buildings are crumbling shambles. In 2008, Obama friend and fundraiser Rezko was convicted on sixteen counts of corruption, including scheming to get kickbacks out of money management firms wanting state business, wire and mail fraud, and aiding and abetting bribery. Happily, he was acquitted on extortion charges.

Obama's choice of friends certainly could lead to questions about his judgment. But on closer scrutiny, Obama's behavior is entirely consistent with a diagnosis of narcissism. The unsavory assortment of characters in Obama's life—Ayers, Rezko, Wright, et al.—each performed some essential service in furthering the future president's political aspirations.

When narcissism is coupled with another form of pathology—that is, when the narcissist is also a psychopath or antisocial—it makes for potentially dangerous people. Dr. Vaknin describes the "malignant narcissist" as having pathological narcissism. The pathological narcissist will subtly misrepresent facts, or what we call in the political context, a flip-flop. Lacking a solid core of principles makes it easy to switch positions as required. (10)

The malignant narcissist carries a messianic vision of himself and is prone to magical thinking, that is, he ignores data that conflicts with his fantasy. (11) Perhaps along the lines of establishing the nonexistent office of the president-elect complete with seal?

How is it a young man in his forties with virtually no accomplishments felt compelled to write not one but *two* autobiographies? The University of Chicago paid Obama a fellowship to write a book about race relations. Instead, he wrote a book about himself. (12) Hitler wrote an autobiography when he was just thirty-five.

Telegraph reporter Stephanie Gutmann describes her reaction to Obama's appearance in Berlin: "After it was over I picked up the phone and called a friend back home. 'It's worse than we thought,' I told him. 'The guy's actually crazy.'" (13) Guttman was talking about candidate Obama's agenda as he presented it that day, in which he promised to take on the terrorists in Afghanistan, take on the drug dealers, rebuild Afghanistan, eliminate the building nuclear threat, secure all loose nukes, decrease arsenals from another era, form a new global partnership that will end terror networks, redistribute wealth, save the planet, withdraw all troops from Iraq, keep the oceans from rising, end famine, and reduce carbon output. (14)

Most politicians would have quit after two or three such ambitious proposals.

Pretty big talk from a politician who, two months into his new administration, does not even have a functioning treasury department. The Berlin speech was an excellent example of Obama's grandiosity. Most candidates for the US presidency limit their campaign to the United States and her territories. Obama felt compelled to take his campaign to Europe, carrying on as if he were a true head of state and indulging in wildly magical thinking about his agenda.

These are not the behaviors of a healthy, balanced personality. To be charitable, Obama is not the only narcissist in politics. Indeed, the nature of American politics makes it unlikely that anyone without some narcissistic traits would run for office. Again, it's a matter of degree. There is something grandiose, by definition, in waking up one morning and deciding that you are qualified to be the leader of the free world. It is a bit unusual to throw your hat in the ring in the fourth grade, as did Obama. He was going to school in Indonesia at the time, so the record isn't clear as to what country he planned to rule.

Beyond the Obvious

The inherent problem in putting a narcissist in the White House is having a president who will always put his own needs ahead of the welfare of the country. The prevaricator-in-chief could, under the right circumstances, be dangerous. The narcissist's life revolves around maintaining a steady narcissistic supply. Inside the true narcissist, there really is "no there, there." He exists only by reflection. Again, Bill Clinton is an excellent example of the species. As Peggy Noonan recently pointed out, Clinton had the ability to figure out exactly who he needed to be to win over his audience and could adapt himself accordingly.

Many domestic abusers are narcissists, depending on their partners for their narcissistic fixes. When a wife or girlfriend fails by not living up to his fantasy of his dream woman, the narcissist experiences rage. This is why a batterer can blow up over something inconsequential. If his wife didn't get a chance to clean the house, it becomes a narcissistic injury to the abuser; after all, he married the perfect wife and is entitled to a perfectly clean house. Some abusers experience narcissistic rage when their partner becomes pregnant; again, she isn't dream girl anymore, and a new baby may steal her attention. Experts in domestic abuse universally agree that a battered woman is in the most danger when she attempts to end the relationship. She is threatening to cut off the abuser's narcissistic supply; this is when he will be at his most enraged and most dangerous.

The narcissist in chief has been needling private citizens on talk radio and Fox News for insufficient veneration. The leader of the free world is impelled to use his standing to rebuke talk radio hosts while Iran is on fire, his economic policies are having catastrophic effects on jobs, and lunatics in North Korea are planning to launch a missile at Hawaii.

For the narcissist, nothing matters more than maintaining his supply. From Obama's perspective, being criticized by a cable news commentator really is a bigger threat than the possibility of Iran getting nuclear weapons.

The current leader of the free world is not in touch with reality. The toady press gleefully accepts his fabrications and denials. And mental health professionals have shown a remarkable lack of curiosity about the mental health of the president of the United States.

We are all born narcissists. An infant is completely fixated on his own survival; he is forced to depend on others to meet his needs, and he is absorbed entirely with addressing fundamental drives such as hunger and discomfort. (15) The infant lacks the ability to identify his own primary emotions; until these emotions are recognized, they can't be modulated or understood.

At approximately six months, the infant begins to differentiate the self, and the attention starts to shift beyond his own body boundaries. (16) Eventually, through interactions with others, the infant starts to recognize basic emotions. If the child's needs are consistently met, he establishes trust in the caregiver and develops his own sense of self-worth.

According to Dr. Peter Fonagy, the role of the mother in this developmental process is *crucial*. Mothers teach their infants how to study the outside world and other people, as well as putting emotions in context. (17) Child psychiatrist Donald Winnicott says that a healthy mother mirrors the child's behavior back to him by way of her own behavior, which signals to the child that she recognizes and appreciates his emotional state. She underscores and validates the infant's experience of the world with appropriate holding, stroking, and other shows of acceptance and affection. (18) Through this process, the child learns to identify his own feelings.

Learning to recognize one's own feelings is essential as it forms the basis for learning to regulate conduct and connect with others. Developmentally, the child must learn to identify, manage, and exchange emotions (19).

Ideally, self-recognition leads to the ability to monitor one's own feelings and thoughts and *the ability to understand the thoughts and feelings of others*. This is the foundation for the evolution of empathy. As the capacity for empathy grows, the child's natural grandiose belief that he is the center of the universe recedes. (20)

When this early primary form of emotional interaction malfunctions, there is the possibility of trauma. The child who doesn't get the necessary validation and mirroring from his mother may misinterpret or disregard his own feelings, which leads later to an inability to connect with others, as well as difficulty regulating his own emotions. (21)

If the trauma is extreme or ongoing, the child may experience the ultimate disconnection known as dissociation. Dissociation is a complete disconnect from one's own feelings; at its most extreme, it can feel like an out-of-body experience or a sense of numbness. Repeated trauma can actually block the brain's normal growth. (22)

It is remarkably easy to disrupt this developmental process if the mother is unavailable for any reason either due to physical absence or emotional detachment. The presence of an engaged and loving mother is most crucial up to the age of twelve if the child is to develop a capacity for healthy social functioning. (23)

When trauma occurs prior to the age of twelve, the child typically blames himself, believing he caused the traumatic event. This is the child's way of making sense out of events he cannot possibly understand. But this mistaken belief also leads to feelings of grandiosity, which may become fixed. (24) Without healthy interaction with his mother, the child learns that his feelings don't matter, and in turn, the feelings of others don't matter either. Thus, the child fails to develop normal empathy. *The lack of a sense of self is the hallmark of narcissism.*

We know that Obama's early years were marked by extreme chaos, and a mother who may have been well intentioned was manifestly unprepared to have a child. Recall that Obama's final abandonment by his mother occurred when he was just ten years old.

Chapter 9

Uncle Frankie

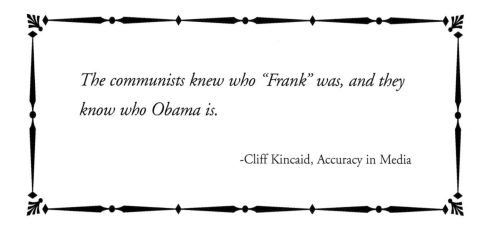

> *The communists knew who "Frank" was, and they know who Obama is.*
>
> -Cliff Kincaid, Accuracy in Media

In a lifetime of associations of nearly exclusively unsavory characters, poet and pornographer Frank Marshall Davis ranks among the least savory of the lot.

Davis was a communist, poet, alcoholic, sexual deviant, and fomenter of racial hatred. Cleverly disguised as Frank in *Dreams,* we learn that young Barry was treated to Davis's counsel on numerous occasions. Dear Grandpa Stanley, blessed with an inordinate amount of free time, thanks to his wife's hard work, enjoyed whiling away the hours with Davis, drinking and smoking pot.

In yet another series of twists and loops, Davis was born in Kansas, as were the Dunhams. It is not entirely clear whether Davis and Dunham knew each other in Kansas. Davis, an unabashed admirer of the Soviet Union, member of the Communist Party USA (CPUSA), and fomenter of racial hatred, worked as a columnist in Chicago, where he fancied himself someone of great importance.

In 1948, Davis moved to Hawaii with his second wife, socialite Helen Canfield, (1) at the suggestion of actor and communist Paul Robeson. Davis immediately took up the cause of the International Longshore and Warehouse Union (ILWU), an organization in which every member was also a member of CPUSA, and formed an unbroken chain from China to the University of Hawaii's Department of Ethnic Studies. (2) ILWU was entirely controlled by members of the Communist Party and, in turn, ran the Democratic Party in Hawaii.

Davis began writing a column for the *Honolulu Record*, the union newspaper. He was never able to make much of a name for himself as a writer in Hawaii. In fact, the paper didn't see fit to actually pay him for his subversive writings.

The *Record* was founded following the convictions of ILWU chief Jack Hall and *Record* editor Koji Ariyoshi in 1953 of "conspiring to teach and advocate the overthrow of the government by force and violence." (3) The convictions were eventually reversed in 1958 after the court reinterpreted the Smith Act.

Obama's grandparents moved the family to Hawaii in 1959, and Stanley Dunham made, or renewed, his friendship with super patriot Davis.

The two had plenty in common other than their success in work avoidance. Both men were strongly left-leaning drinkers who enjoyed whiling away the hours, looking for ways to increase racial tensions on the island.

Davis was an open supporter of the Soviet Union and his influence on Obama is hard to miss. The poet also admitted to writing a pornographic novel under the pseudonym of Bob Greene, in which the protagonist seduces a thirteen-year-old girl. Davis claimed he had changed names and identities, but the novel was based on actual experiences. To clarify the depth of Marshall's perversion, he actually believed sex with a thirteen-year-old child would be in the child's best interests. He graciously spared her the sting of rejection and made certain her earliest sexual experiences would be with the maestro himself, according to Toby Harnden in the *The Daily Telegraph*. (4) Davis also proudly proclaimed himself bisexual, a voyeur and exhibitionist who wished he'd had two penises.

Davis was an important mentor to Obama, and he shared his special version of how to improve race relations: never trust white people. Davis died in 1987, but was eventually replaced by Reverend Jeremiah Wright.

Obama's earliest visits to dear Uncle Frank began when Barry was just a vulnerable young boy of ten. Already confused and traumatized by his chaotic childhood, who better to step up to the role of big brother than a race-bating, America-hating, rabid sexual deviant and pornographer?

Davis's support of the Soviet Union and the Communist Party was so extreme that he was rejected by the NAACP in Chicago, not exactly a conservative organization, out of fears that his extremism would drive new members away.

> "There are other 'critics of racism' who got a taste of the Communists' tactics from Davis. A 1949 letter sent to NAACP acting National Secretary Roy Wilkins by a Honolulu attorney and NAACP leader named Edward Berman:
>
> "I was at one of the election meetings at which one Frank Marshall Davis, formerly of Chicago (and formerly editor of the Chicago Communist paper, the Star) suddenly appeared on the scene to propagandize the membership about our 'racial problems' in Hawaii. He had just sneaked in here on a boat, and presto, was an 'expert' on racial problems in Hawaii. Comrade Davis was supported by others who had recently 'sneaked' into the organization with the avowed intent and purpose of converting it into a front for the Stalinist line...
>
> "...Already, scores of Negro members were frightened away from these meetings because of the influx of this element. Only by a reorganization with a policy that will check this infiltration, can we hope to get former members back into a local NAACP branch. We are going to have to have that authority over here—otherwise you'll have a branch exclusively composed of yelping Stalinists and their dupes—characters

who are more concerned about the speedy assassination of Tito
(who had just broken with the USSR) than they are about the
advancement of the colored people of these United States."

Shortly after receiving this letter, the NAACP revoked its Honolulu Chapter's charter in order to reorganize and prevent a Communist takeover of the organization. (5)

In 1956, Davis had exercised his Fifth Amendment right against self-incrimination while being investigated by the House Un-American Activities Committee (HUAC). He chose to remain silent rather than acknowledge the excruciatingly obvious—that he was a communist. (6)

By extrapolation, we can presume that Grandpa Stanley's views were in synch with Davis's, given the amount of time the men spent getting loaded together and having long drunken arguments. (7)

In 1950, Davis wrote a column entitled "Free Enterprise or Socialism?" hoping that America was at a turning point, a perfect storm, so to speak, that would allow him and his comrades to finally trash the free enterprise system and replace it with something else. "Of course, they could not fully disclose themselves, their beliefs, and their intentions, although any thinking observer could easily read between the lines. The key was to gain the support of the people who didn't know the difference." (8)

Davis believed it was capitalism, unregulated by government and run amok, which caused the Great Depression. Obama seems to have picked up this lesson pretty well. A Stalinist to the cellular level, Davis blamed all the evils in the world on the United States. The future ACORN fell close to the tree.

Nothing will drive the Left into a paroxysm like the mere mention of communist influences in the United States. No matter how much evidence has piled up over the decades about subversive cabals operating in the United States to infiltrate our government at all levels, the mere suggestion that the communists were ever a threat to our national security is invariably met with wild derision. At some point, the invective McCarthyism will be spat at the offender with an indignant sense of finality as if no further discussion could be tolerated without complete destruction of the fabric of decent society.

Liberals have been embarrassing themselves for decades with this McCarthy business. Point out an unsavory association, and they squeal like stuck pigs about the scourge of McCarthyism. In the mind of the liberal, Senator McCarthy was a deranged conservative finding imaginary communists under every rock and creating the fiction of the Red Menace. Note: they have the same attitude today about critics of radical Islam.

Following the fall of the Soviet Union in the 1990s, enormous amounts of data became available, including the *Verona* papers: coded messages from the KGB and other communist intelligence agencies about communist agents in the United States. (9)

We also know now that CPUSA was a faithful creature of the Soviet Union. "Far from being mere indigenous radicals working for peace and social justice, as sometimes argued, the party and its members were subservient tools of Moscow-and those who weren't subversive didn't stay very long as members." (10)

From a composite of all these data, it's evident the Soviet/Communist operation in the United States, as elsewhere, was vast, sophisticated, and effective, nowhere more so than in seeking positions of official influence. The Red networks reached into virtually every important aspect of the US government, up to very high levels, the State Department notably included. All of which was obviously congruent with the warnings of McCarthy and others who sounded the alarm about such matters in the late 1940s and early '50s. There was in fact an immense conspiracy afoot, there were secret Communists burrowing in the woodwork, and these Communists were, in case after case, devoted agents of the Soviet Union. (11)

Obama, evidently, has not yet been brought up to speed on the *Verona* project and other new information. He refers to McCarthyism as "cowardice" in *Dreams*. (12) McCarthy didn't vote "present" on matters of national security.

As is the nature of liberals, the introduction of facts changes nothing; and they persist in their endless bleating about McCarthyism each and every time one of Obama's deeply disturbing mentor's names comes up.

Along with the extraordinary political science and American history education provided by Davis, we would be remiss to overlook the pornographer's contribution to young Barry's social development. "He stated that 'under certain circumstances, I am bisexual' and that he was 'a voyeur and an exhibitionist' who was 'occasionally interested in sadomasochism,' adding, 'I have often wished I had two penises to enjoy simultaneously the double but different sensations of oral and genital copulation." (13) So says the favored mentor of Obama, future president of the United States.

Stanley Dunham's relationship with Davis reflects an appalling lack of appropriate boundaries. If two grown ne'er-do-wells chose to waste their time drinking, smoking pot, and spewing hate, so be it; but as the alleged adult, Dunham was way out of line exposing a child of ten to such an influence as Frank Marshall Davis.

We likely will never know all of the details of each meeting between Obama and Davis over the years. Obama himself may not have entirely accurate recollections; such is the nature of extreme experiences in childhood. The very best we can say is that his grandfather failed to provide a healthy role model for the impressionable child. Exposing a child to race hating, communist ideology, along with all manners of sexual perversion, is child abuse and can be expected to have lasting consequences.

Chapter 10

Saul Alinsky: Master Agitator

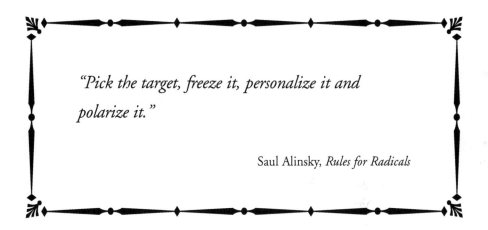

"Pick the target, freeze it, personalize it and polarize it."

Saul Alinsky, *Rules for Radicals*

All practicing Leftists have been influenced by Saul Alinsky, author of *Rules for Radicals*, the essential primer for all good America-hating radicals. Written by the great granddaddy of all community organizers, Alinsky's book lays out the tactics to be employed in creating a revolution.

When I was growing up in Chicago in the 1960s, these folks were known as "paid agitators," a far more accurate description of what they do. Community organizers were carpetbaggers who blew into town for the express purpose of whipping the locals into frenzy over some grievance, real or imagined. This type of "organizing" is not to be compared with legitimate, local, grassroots organizations that get together to put pressure on local officials to bring about a change for the better. Alinsky-style organizers are not concerned members of the community who pressure city hall into putting in a new stoplight. For the Alinskyite, the actual issue is of no consequence. The organizer doesn't care about the community. The agenda is to gin up a revolt, which gives the organizer *power*. As Alinsky put it, "You want to cause fear, confusion, and retreat in the enemy, i.e. the Haves." (2) Remember Hoffer's work on mass movements: the organizer's task is to inject the society with an ailment and then offer the movement as the cure. "Agitate, aggravate, educate, then organize." (3)

As is always the case with socialism, Alinsky's programs never succeeded. Barack Obama's lack of success as a community organizer is what motivated him to pursue a law degree.

By all accounts, Obama was a model Alinsky student; evidently, results are not considered in the grading process. In actual practice, the results of Obama's agitating were less than spectacular. He organized the residents of the Altgeld Gardens public housing project to have dangerous asbestos removed. It was a small victory, at best. Workers sealed the asbestos in some units but quickly abandoned the project. Some tenants still have asbestos today. A $500,000 initiative for a jobs bank was a flop. Despite a few bright moments, overall, Obama's community organizing was ineffective in bringing any genuine help to the people he claimed to want to represent. Obama had the benefit of receiving his training from disciples who had studied with Alinsky himself; he went on to train hundreds of others in Alinskyism. Obama has said that his Alinsky training was the best education of his life. A former fellow organizer told the *New Republic* that Obama was the "undisputed master" of agitation. (4)

Phyllis Schlafly points out, "The organizer's first job is to create the issues or problems, and the organization must be based on many issues," and [the organizer] must first rub raw the resentments of the people of the community; fan the latent hostilities of many of the people to the point of overt action." (5) Sounds like a description of a paid agitator, doesn't it?

What distinguished Alinsky from your run-of-the-mill revolutionary is Alinsky's preference to wreck the system from within the existing order rather than resort to violence, not that violence is out of the question, however. Alinsky was a big believer in the end justifying the means.

Saul Alinsky also subscribed to a style of ethics that has been described as "very fluid." In other words, there is no right or wrong in any absolute sense. Marxists despise religion, the original source of morality; the Marxist has substituted the state for the church. The future president's mentor didn't believe integrity was an important quality, but creating the *illusion* of integrity is essential. (6)

Alinsky wanted organizers to infiltrate the middle classes by learning to blend in and not scare them off with the vulgarity and coarseness that was typical of the Ayers-style radicals. (7) Bill Ayers eventually caught on as well and figured out how to inject himself into academia. Alinskyites were trained to work their way into existing institutions: churches, unions, schools, and other institutions. (8)

Just how does one qualify for Alinsky training? He had specific traits he wanted to see in his pupils; number one and most important, ego. Alinsky believed the best organizers were the ones driven to play God, who were irreverent, could demonstrate a sense of humor and had confidence. (9) Undeniably, Obama was just the kind of guy Alinsky was looking for.

Alinsky disciples were trained to decide what they needed and wanted and then cover it up using the language of morality, like pretending to be working for peace. (10) The organizer was to generate crises and grab power.

Alinsky's favorite word? "Change." Change to what who knows? It doesn't matter. Alinsky people don't really bother themselves with the end game. They are preoccupied with agitating the population to manufacture crises, which allow them to seize power. Alinsky doesn't really provide much guidance as to what to do after the revolution. "The organizer's biggest job is to give the people the feeling they can do something."(11) "If the communists had been able to take over Europe and beyond, it would have been because of their knowledge of how to preach hope."(12)

Does any of this hope-and-change verbiage sound a bit familiar? Yet again, we pull back the curtain only to find Obama's lack of originality. Whip the people into a frenzy, create a crisis, then offer hope and change—that's the blueprint.

We have seen more Alinskyisms since Obama became a candidate, as when he called out conservative talk show hosts Sean Hannity and Rush Limbaugh. Obama's anti-Limbaugh campaign began shortly after taking the highest office in the land. Understanding Alinskyism helps explain this ignominious behavior: "Ridicule is man's most potent weapon. It is almost impossible to counterattack ridicule." (13) No match for Limbaugh's linguistic jujitsu skills, the best efforts of a White House cabal, including leftover left-wing political hacks from the Clinton administration, managed to boost Limbaugh's ratings and introduce him to the curious. It is astounding that Obama is using the White House to harass private citizens. But Obama surely would have earned a gold star if Alinsky was still with us. L. David Alinsky, son of Saul, submitted a letter to the *Boston Globe*, which was published, extolling the virtues of Dad's star pupil. Right after the Democratic National Convention, Alinsky Jr. wrote, "I am proud to see that my father's model for organizing is being applied successfully beyond local community organizing to affect the Democratic campaign in 2008. It is a fine tribute to Saul Alinsky as we approach his 100th birthday." (14)

What's not to be proud of? Daddy Alinsky taught the importance of creating moral confusion and public discontent to achieve a takeover. There were to be no peaceful solutions and no compromises; the task is to totally crush and transform society. (15) Alinsky had this to say about the middle class, "Insecure in a fast changing world, they cling to illusory fixed points which are very real to them." (16) Yet another striking example of Obama's skill in parroting others—recall his comments in San Francisco about "bitter clingers" with their guns and religion. Originality is not an Obama virtue.

Alinsky's writings don't seem to be anchored in any core values or principles; Alinsky training is about agitating the masses and overthrowing the current order. Alinsky taught that all problems are caused by capitalism. We can see his little protégé currently doing his darnedest to dismantle our free market system at warp speed.

ACORN Seeds

In the 1960s, two other Alinsky grads and Columbia sociologists, Andrew Cloward and Frances Fox Piven, devised a scheme to bring about the downfall of capitalism by overloading government bureaucracy with a flood of impossible demands. (17)

Drawing inspiration from the highly successful Watts riots in 1965, they wrote that the current welfare system provided a social safety net, which only doused the fires of rebellion. Cloward and Piven believed that the poor would only advance if the rest of society was afraid of them. When the system inevitably failed, use that failure to discredit the system. They organized a mass movement to load up the welfare rolls to the breaking point. They first used these "shock troops" in 1975 to flood the welfare rolls in New York City. The scheme worked; New York City went bankrupt and sought a federal bailout. (18) Eventually, Rudy Giuliani had to clean up the mess.

Cloward and Piven were big fans of the Trojan Horse movement, that is, a mass movement with an ostensibly legitimate purpose with the true agenda of drafting the poor into service for the revolution. (19) The grand strategy was to use poor people as cannon fodder to tear down the capitalist system. (20)

The same tactics were later applied to elections. The idea was to swamp the voter rolls with invalid registrations; new "voting rights" coalitions were formed to yell "racism" and "disenfranchisement" at every opportunity. Teams of lawyers were brought in to file frivolous lawsuits. (21) Clinton's 1993 Motor Voter law was a dream come true for radicals.

The Association of Community Organizations for Reform Now (ACORN) was a perfect fit for Alinsky's moral relativism. In 1993, ACORN recruited Obama for Project Vote, an ACORN front group. In 1995, Obama represented ACORN, and he filed suit on their behalf in Illinois over the Motor Voter law. This would appear to be the sum total of Obama's legal career.

In 1996, Obama filled out a questionnaire listing groups that would provide him with key support. Number one on the list? ACORN. The list was not alphabetical. (22)

ACORN is an openly radical group with an annual budget of over $40 million. In the 1970s, they discovered a pot of gold in the Community Reinvestment Act, filing complaints and delaying or killing bank mergers, thereby forcing them into formal agreements with ACORN. (23) ACORN dragooned lenders to make mortgage loans to borrowers without the means to repay them and were a key factor in the sub-prime mortgage crisis.

ACORN's voter registration chicanery is legendary. "Much of the mischief involving voter registration fraud efforts seem to originate from ACORN."(24)

It's no wonder Obama presses for funding for ACORN. "ACORN runs 'Camp O,'" according to John Fund, who has done extensive research on voter fraud. "Stop thinking about Barack Obama and be Barack Obama," says Jocelyn Woods, summing up a two-day training program for ACORN applicants. (25)

The lesson Obama seems to have absorbed best is "pick the target, freeze it, personalize it, and polarize it."(26) Early in his presidency, Obama chose Rush Limbaugh as his target of choice. By selecting a target and zeroing in on it, the target's supporters will come out of the woodwork to support the target, which allows the effective revolutionary to identify who the enemies are. That allows for polarization; that is, if you are not for us, you are against us. The mission is to get the enemy to react, which gives the revolutionary a measure of power and control over the prey. (27) Alinsky doesn't address this directly, but it would seem prudent to avoid selecting targets that are smarter than you are. Limbaugh deftly and entirely predictably turned Obama's provocation into a ratings bonanza.

Following the Alinsky party line, the White House Limbaugh Aspersion Committee launched a ridicule campaign against the popular conservative radio host. Alinsky alums understand that laughing at the enemy is more potent than making threats.

Former CBS newsman Bernard Goldberg told Hannity that the Obama administration's attempt to make Rush the face of the Republican Party would appeal to less sophisticated moderates and independents. (28) The more discerning among us have known for a while that Republican candidates rarely listen to Limbaugh's counsel. The elections of 2006 and 2008 corroborate this.

Does the president of the United States have nothing better to do than harass private citizens who criticize his policies?

Obama's entire campaign and presidency pay homage to professional purveyor of agitation Saul Alinsky. Nary an original idea ever seems to enter the mind of Obama. Byron York sums it up: "Obama applied his considerable organizational skills to perpetuating the old, failed ways of doing things." (29)

Chapter 11

George Soros: International Man of Misery

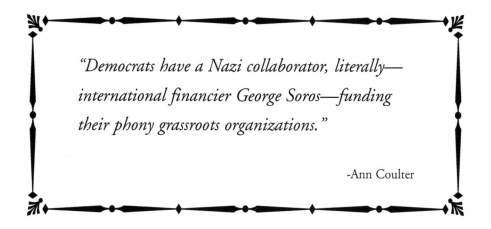

"Democrats have a Nazi collaborator, literally—
international financier George Soros—funding
their phony grassroots organizations."

-Ann Coulter

The term "euphemism" refers to the substitution of a vague or milder term for one that may be considered harsh, offensive, or blunt.

Example:

George Soros is a philanthropist.

If by "philanthropist" we mean one who creates chaos, destruction, and financial ruin for his own personal gain, it's a perfect fit. Calling Soros a philanthropist is rather like referring to the Nazi block wardens as neighborhood watch.

Soros certainly gives lots of money away. But a philanthropist acts to improve the human condition. Soros acts solely to improve the Soros condition. Despite the lofty-sounding rhetoric about an open society, Soros's objective is to wreck the United States. The concept arose in the 1930s with the notion of a moral code based on "universal principles." After tweaking the concept to suit his own purposes, Soros adopted his own version of an open society, which would be one in which the United States has no power. For those with an abundance of stamina, Soros has written several largely-unreadable books in which he references himself excessively and provides rambling explanations of his visions.

Soros was born in Hungary in 1930 to nonpracticing Jewish parents. His father, a lawyer, was able to hide their identities, and young George was recruited by the Judenrat to hand out flyers deceptively directing Jews to turn themselves in for deportation to the death camps. Soros later said he found the work exhilarating. Later passing himself off as an official's godson, he accompanied his benefactor in confiscating valuables from innocent Jews. (1)

Soros would later tell Steve Kroft on *60 Minutes* that he had no remorse about what he had done.

In fact, Soros doesn't have remorse for much, if anything. In the *Shadow Party*, Horowitz and Poe quote Soros as saying that conscience clouds an investor's judgment. (2)

There is little doubt that growing up during Hitler's reign affected young George, but ostensibly not in ways such upheaval would impact a human with a conscience.

"The lessons George Soros learned in WWII were simple and crude. He saw his father's (and his own) law-of-the-jungle morality conquer both the Nazis and death, all the while observing that obeying God's laws caused his fellow Jews to perish-ignominiously, he must have felt. An aging George Soros, to this day, feels no guilt (interview with Steve Kroft; *60 Minutes*, December, 1998) regarding his own complicity in the Nazi's crimes against humanity, however small it may have been and young though he was. He finds no place among those Holocaust survivors blaming themselves for the deaths of others." (3)

In the 1998 interview with Steve Kroft, Soros acknowledged forging documents and pretending to be Christian to save himself, for which he feels no guilt or sorrow. "I was fourteen," Soros said. "My character was made them." Regarding his participation in confiscating valuables from innocent Jews, Soros told Kroft, "It created no problem at all." Soros has no sense that he shouldn't be there; he felt he was a mere spectator. Soros rationalizes his behavior: "If I didn't do it, someone else would." (4)

Predictably, in 2009, as the nation suffers from a protracted recession, causing severe unemployment, the great philanthropist told the *Daily Mail* that he was enjoying a "very good crisis." He boasted about being one of the few people who anticipated the economic meltdown and was able to brace his hedge fund, the Quantum Fund, against the crisis. (5)

Soros amassed his fortune by speculating in the currency markets. He got a lot of attention for tanking the British pound in 1992. More than once, Soros has used his status as an investor to manipulate markets. According to Horowitz and Poe, the great patriot Soros likely sold short after 9/11, when the rest of the nation was being urged to take whatever they could afford and buy some shares of their favorite stocks. Lots of patriotic Americans did exactly that. (6)

To further jeopardize our national security, Soros told CNN that the market would react negatively if the United States were to invade Afghanistan, knowing his words would cause a global market reaction. Soros has stuck his nose in governments all over the world, claiming a philanthropic motive. Soros will adopt a pro- or anti-communist posture, depending on the circumstances. He laughs about "saying one thing in one country and another thing in another." (7)

The Clinton administration allowed Soros to run wild in the dying Soviet Union. The results were entirely predictable. Working in tandem with Strobe Talbott, Russian Policy Czar, they set about playing games with government funds. Soros reveled in having so much access to the Clintons and fancied himself part of the

"Clinton team." Clinton squandered the opportunity to help the Russian people form a healthy democracy and instead allowed Soros and his team to profiteer, leaving the country in shambles. (8)

According to journalist Anne Williamson, Soros appeared before the House Banking Committee in September 1999 attempting to explain to stunned congressmen exactly how so many US taxpayer dollars had evaporated in Russia. The Clintons managed to shut that scandal down quickly, thanks to their expertise in covering up turpitude. (9)

Soros was actually convicted of insider trading in France. His opinion moves markets. He is one of the most powerful people in the world entirely due to his ability to get other people to part with their money. His tentacles are everywhere. He uses numerous foundations and associations to keep money flowing and spread around. It's no secret that George Soros is fond of deceit and subterfuge. He is a radical in the mold of Saul Alinsky. For all of the nonsensical blathering he does about how he can make the world a better place, he has no real plan to do any such thing. Soros loses interest in a project after the demo phase is over. According to Horowitz and Poe, Soros candidly admits he finds destruction easier than creation.

Thus, it makes perfect sense that Soros is the de facto head of the Democratic Party in America now that it is a foaming-at-the-mouth, rabid, left-wing Democratic Party. As Horowitz and Poe put it, "Soros and his Shadow Party did not invent the politics of demagoguery and racial division. They are merely practicing and expanding the politics familiar on the Democratic Left." There is seldom any originality among the left wing.

In 2004, Soros made it his personal mission to defeat George W. Bush. Not only did Bush not share his moral relativism and radical ideology, Soros was outraged about Afghanistan and Iraq. Soros opposed Bush's War on Terror and provided funding to pro-terror groups. Worse still from Soros's point of view, after enjoying easy access to the Clintons, Bush was not equally impressed and failed to seek out his wise counsel on foreign policy.

John Kerry's loss in 2004 was gasoline on the fire. "This is the Sorosization of the Democratic Party," say Rachel Ehrenfelt and Shawn MacComber. "As we will see, this idea of 'scruples' being for the other guy has been central to Soros's philosophy in business, philanthropy, and foreign policy." (10)

Although Soros had a mutually beneficial relationship with the Clintons, he knew enough to hedge his bets in 2008 and back more than one candidate. The type of revolution Soros wants requires a charismatic figure that can create a mass movement. Soros himself actually dislikes publicity. Good oratory skills and personal charisma are what he needs. Soros himself prefers to stay below the radar and work his subterfuge behind the scenes. After all, "Soros's main concern is that somebody be elected who is indebted enough to him to pick up the phone when he calls." (11)

Columnist and former Reagan speechwriter Peggy Noonan recently gave a speech in Indian Wells, California, on the topic of presidents. She told funny stories and shared her insights into Presidents Bush, Reagan, Clinton, and Obama. Noonan talked about Clinton's personal charisma. "It was impossible not to look at him." And his speeches were well delivered but remarkably lacking in substance. Is anyone seeing a pattern here? Noonan sees Obama as more like Clinton than other presidents, not only in his policies but also in his presentation. An early sign that Noonan was recovering from Obamania, she suggested we listen to a soaring Obama speech and then print it out and read the text. Reading a Clinton speech yielded the same letdown.

Is it possible then that Bill Clinton was supposed to fulfill the role of Soros's cult-leading messiah but simply failed at it?

Soros can't wreak his havoc alone. He needs the power of a mass movement. Soros is unquestionably a narcissist, but is short on the charisma.

It's important to understand that Soros doesn't want to "change" America. He wants to destroy it. America in its current state is anathema to Soros. The current Oval Office occupant is not particularly fond of America either. His association with America-hating radicals should be enough for most people, but let's not overlook the fact that his very first sit-down interview after becoming president was to Al Arabiya News Channel. Obama took the opportunity to share his views with the Muslim world that America has behaved very badly, and we can be expected to change our ways so our relationship with Muslims will be like it was "twenty or thirty years ago." This is a bit perplexing unless Obama either knows less about history than we thought, or he longs for the days when Islamofascists led by Khomeini were holding fifty-two American hostages. I daresay the Muslim world was cheered to learn that our new president plans to take us back to the happy, halcyon days of the Carter administration. Soros is actually working toward a plan to completely overhaul the US Constitution.

When Soros gets hold of power in any government, he makes money. It is difficult to find examples of Soros invasions that leave the target country better off. But that is not Soros's concern. Obama's monstrous stimulus bill (euphemisms again) fits neatly into Soros's paradigm. You can read Soros's economy recovery plan on the *Huffington Post* (February 12, 2009).

Most of Obama's stated plans for America are indistinguishable from those of Soros. As the left forces nationalized health care on us, we may want to consider Soros's Project on Death. Soros is a leading promoter of the assisted suicide movement. He papers over it with tripe about compassion; in reality, the project is a push for palliative care rather than treatment for gravely ill patients. As always, it's all about the money:

> Can we afford to care for the dying properly? The number of
> people dying in the United States currently stands at 2.2 million
> annually. Increases in cancer and AIDS and the aging of the baby
> boomers will cause this figure to climb faster than the population
> . . . [Bu] [a]ggressive, life-prolonging interventions, which may at
> times go against the patient's wishes, are much more expensive
> than proper care for the dying. (12)

So said Soros in a 1994 speech. What did he mean by "proper care" for the dying? "This brings me to that hotly debated subject, physician assisted suicide and euthanasia." (13)

Are we ready for Soros care?

Also on the Soros agenda is the creation of worldwide hyperinflation (14); the Obama economic team appears to be racing to make Soros's dream come true.

For all the posturing Soros does about creating his Marxist utopia, there is no actual plan to create a new social order, an open one or otherwise. Soros, for all of his rambling, hasn't thought it through that far, and he is not going to. His interest begins and ends with his potential to exploit whomever he can to grab money and power. He actually makes garden-variety dopey liberals rather endearing by comparison. At least some of them believe in their unrealistic vision of socialism.

When President Obama-Soros commandeers our health care system, aided by congress, be wary of jargon like "involuntary euthanasia." We dodged a bullet with the demolition of Hillarycare, only to find ourselves facing something even more malevolent. As baby boomers age, there is no question that demand for health care services will outstrip supply. At the same time, nationalizing health care creates little incentive for talented students to endure the rigors of medical school, internships and residencies. The rationing of health care is inevitable.

The compassionate Nazi collaborator wants us to believe that his interest in caring for the dying was sparked by the death of his own father. Soros was irked at his father's obstinate refusal to just die already: "...unfortunately [he] wanted to live... I was kind of disappointed in him ... I wrote him off." (15)

In Australia's Northern Territory, Soros has already managed to buy significant government influence leading to reports of patients being pressured into accepting euthanasia. Another inescapable consequence of socialized medicine will be that medical decisions will be made not by doctors and patients, but by somnolent government bureaucrats who themselves have good insurance.

Barack himself acknowledged Soros' geriatricide plan when he responded to a question from Jane Sturm whose 100 year old mother was denied a pacemaker because of her age. Sturm rejected the Soros platform and did not order her mother to lie down and die. Instead, Sturm found a doctor willing to provide the pacemaker, appreciating that Strum's mother was not in the mood to expire on command. It was a revelation to Mr. Obama that some seniors enjoy a high quality of life and can remain spry.

The Narcissist in Chief, who is afflicted with a sepulchral lack of empathy replied:

"I don't think that we can make judgments based on peoples' spirit," Obama said. "That would be a pretty subjective decision to be making. I think we have to have rules that say that we are going to provide good, quality care for all people. "

Dr. Obama suggested that one expeditious way to curtail medical costs is to for you to forgo having surgery and take a painkiller instead. Is that really a decision you want the Pelosi- led government to make for you or your loved ones? The Termination Team will be delighted to make the opiate of the masses an actual opiate. A drugged up populace is easier to subjugate.

Also noteworthy was Obama's position that he wanted the finest possible care for his own family, thus he can't seriously be expected to use Obama-Soros care himself. Nor do we expect the members of Congress, despite their manifest dispensability, to abdicate their superlative coverage to sign up with the rest of the peasants.

"If you like your doctor, you will be able to keep your doctor, period. If you like your health care plan, you will be able to keep your health care plan, period," Obama promised last week. Obama's record on keeping promises is well chronicled. It's amazing that some people still listen to his palaver as if it had some substance.

Soros' depraved attitude toward his father's will to live was not the only catalyst for his Death Project. It was also stoked by the abject failure of Hillarycare; another odious and ill-conceived program that was fortunately derailed as soon as the public found out what it was. Soros, determined not to let that happen again, set about bankrolling the inglorious McCain-Feingold bill, a campaign finance "reform" law that nobody but Soros wanted. Using phony research polls, Soros was able to sell the hoax that the American people were desperate for campaign finance reform. The creation of 527 organizations essentially allowed George Soros to purchase the Democrat Party, albeit somewhat stealthily. David Horowitz and Richard Poe correctly refer to Soros as head of the Shadow Party, a party within the Democrat Party. The Shadow Party is now unmistakably ruling the country.

Liberals have been priming us for socialized medicine for years. The left loathes drug companies with a fervor normally reserved for beauty queens and executives.

If we fail to abort Obama-Soros care, "involuntary euthanasia" will become part of standard medical treatment.

Keeping in mind that Soros will always act in ways that provide maximum benefit to Soros, what are his plans for Obama? It's clear he found the cult leader he needed. Obama is performing correctly with his daily catastrophizing and power grabbing. But what would benefit Soros more, a successful Obama presidency or a failed one? Success would give Soros four to eight years to work in the shadows to destroy America and grab what spoils he can. Obama and his Ministry of Propaganda have managed to create fear and panic in the population. His policies, if implemented, cannot but lead to economic trouble and eventual shortages and rationing. Nobody knows more about how to destroy a currency than Soros. We have to question whether the peculiar short-selling patterns in the fall of 2008 and the overhyped economic "collapse" were staged to get Obama elected. If an inept, inexperienced, and radical president has his way, which Obama surely will, the net result is pretty predictable. Is that kind of social and economic chaos designed to open up a power vacuum that a guy like Soros just can't resist?

Chapter 12

Depraved Cult Leaders of Yore

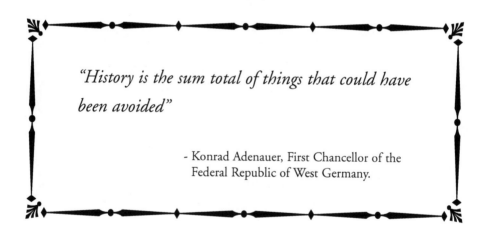

"History is the sum total of things that could have been avoided"

- Konrad Adenauer, First Chancellor of the
Federal Republic of West Germany.

I can remember the feeling I had when he spoke. At last, I said, here's somebody who can get us out of this mess. (1)

He was so convincing on the speaker's platform and appeared to be so sincere in what he said that the majority of his listeners were ready to believe almost anything good about him because they wanted to believe it. (2)

As time went on, it became clear that he thought of himself as the Messiah. (3)

He was the greatest orator Germany had ever known. (4) Most amazing of all: he did it without a teleprompter. The comparisons between Hitler and Obama, while offensive to many, were inevitable. They both had the benefit of oratory skills and could deliver a stirring speech with minimal substance. They pitched the same slogan, "Everything must change!" (5)

Hitler used the Great Depression as his chance to seize power. The chanting, sloganeering, and fainting crowds—we've seen this all before, and the outcome wasn't very constructive. It would be temerarious to fail to study the history of other cult leaders who rose to power at breakneck speed. The same Great Depression allowed FDR to get away with making radical changes in America.

A troubled childhood seems to be a prerequisite for future cult leaders. Alice Miller calls child-rearing practices in turn of the century Germany as "the concealed concentration camp of childhood." (6) Miller theorizes that Hitler's father's brutality led to the acting out of repressed revenge fantasies, which can lead to "indescribable atrocities." Abused children feel powerless, and murderous thugs like Hitler compensate for those feelings by becoming masters of violence. (7)

In attestation to the incompetence of our public school system, liberals never tire of claiming that Hitler was the ultimate right-winger. As usual, they are completely wrong. Hitler's party was the National *Socialist* German Workers' Party. Liberals are always screeching about how conservatives are fascists. Jonah Goldberg does a masterful job of describing the fascist playbook:

- Create crises.
- Make appeals for "unity."
- Celebrate martial values.
- Blur the lines between the public and private sectors.
- Use the mainstream media to glamorize the state and its programs.

- Make a lot of noise about "post partisanship."
- Form a cult of personality around the national leader. (8)

Goldberg has provided a pretty good description of the Barack Obama platform. Conservatives are not fascists. True conservatives place the highest value on individual liberty, which is as irreconcilable with the current liberal agenda as it was with Hitler's Nazism.

The tenderhearted Führer was also a champion of animal rights. Adolf may have originated the entire concept of political correctness: a nice day was to be referred to as "Hitler weather"; one way in which Hitler was able to change the values and frequencies of words. (9)

Adolf Hitler was certainly a proponent of what we now call identity politics, a destructive process by which liberals dissect the population into groups. Thus, we have a gay community, an African American community, a Hispanic community, and various and sundry other labels, limited only by the liberal imagination. Note that liberals never talk about an American community. Dividing the country into artificial groups allows the liberal Left to create imaginary victims and oppressors. This is what liberals call multiculturalism. Barack Obama got quite a boost from these liberal fictions; by the power of liberal guilt, Obama was, by definition, the superior candidate by virtue of his race. Most conservatives recall Dr. Martin Luther King's appeal to judge a man by the content of his character rather than the color of his skin. We said okay. It is liberals who think racial color blindness is a form of racism. (10) In point of fact, there are so few conservative racists that liberals have had to invent pretend code words and then try to catch conservatives using them in their tireless effort to keep grievances alive. Like all tyrants, liberals govern through fear. (11) It is almost farcical to note that Hitler accused other parties of being "divisive" along sectarian lines and insisted he only wanted to focus on the economy. (12)

Hitler believed all institutions should work together as if they were part of some machine; this included using private businesses for his own purposes and propaganda. He was able to manipulate the press and the film industry.

Liberals should be jubilant to learn that Hitler also declared war on tobacco and alcohol; pushed new food certifications; and, foreshadowing our future bureaucracies, created industrial hygienists to develop workplace safety regulations.

Upon becoming chancellor, Hitler told the *New York Times* that his number one priority was ending unemployment; nothing else mattered but creating jobs. (13) Germany after World War I was a mess, the government was corrupt, the citizens were dispirited, and the economy was collapsing. The Germans were also nervous about the new and militant Soviet Union after Lenin overthrew the czar. (14) The German people didn't have much faith in democracy. "They longed for a strong leader who promised them jobs and a better life even if he had extreme ideas."(15)

Once again, we find the perfect storm, that ideal confluence of factors that enables a cult figure to grab power and exploit it. Adolf Hitler was a man of minimal accomplishment and skill and a failed artist. Hitler studied public speaking and psychology but was born too early to have the benefit of Alinsky training.

Hitler had plenty of help from the mainstream press, which he used as his own propaganda machine, which portrayed him as "extra human." Once Hitler rose to power, the propaganda machine inflated everything he did right. Tight control of the press kept the public's understanding of Hitler to a minimum. His appearances were staged to create feelings of the supernatural and religious. Can we really be expected to avoid comparisons to Obama's fake Greek columns for his speech at the Democratic Convention? The German people came to see Hitler as a messiah. Portraits appeared with halos, and comparisons were made to Jesus. (16) Hitler also understood the importance of disarming the citizenry if he were to seize control of the nation. As Dave Kopel of *National Review Online* explains it, "Simply put, without gun control, Hitler would not have been able to murder 21 million people." (17)

> "Women faint, when with face purpled and contorted with effort, he blows forth his magic oratory." (18)

Hitler was able to tap a source of cheap labor when he formed his youth corps. He understood kids as a political force; membership in the Hitler youth gave them *hope* and a chance to be heard. (15) Young people were required to serve for six months following high school graduation. They were put to work farming, road building, and other projects. (19) You know, "infrastructure."

The Hitler youth were not always aware of what was going on, nor were the movement's victims: "We, the young fanatics of the Hitler Youth, had also become the Führer's victims… They [the Jews] often didn't know they were going to die until the last few minutes." (20) However, at least some of the young people were told by senior officers or figured it out. Some historians believe it is preposterous that anyone living in Germany at the time of Hitler could have been oblivious. Still, the young Hitler fanatic did not always accept the truth. (21) When shown documentary films of the death camps, many times, the young true believers responded with anger, convinced the films were fakes. (22)

So durable was the hold this cult leader had on his young followers that they were able to block out the unpleasant realties of the Final Solution, even when presented with the truth. Former Hitler Youth member Alfons Heck writes, "It was some time before I could accept the truth of the Holocaust, nearly three decades more before I could write or speak about German guilt and responsibility." (23)

Heck describes the bond he felt with Hitler:

> None of us who reached high rank in the Hitler Youth ever
> totally shake the legacy of the Führer. Despite our monstrous
> sacrifice and the appalling misuse of our idealism, there will
> always be the memory of unsurpassed power, the intoxications
> of fanfares and flags proclaiming our new age. (24)

What Heck describes illustrates the power of the trauma bond. Bonds developed out of trauma tend to be far more durable than healthy bonds. The theory of Stockholm syndrome rests on the tenacity of traumatic bonding. (25)

In 2006, White House chief of staff Rahm Emanuel wrote *The Plan: Big Ideas for America*. Emanuel's plan calls for universal citizen service, asserting that every citizen must do his or her part. Under the plan, young people between the ages of eighteen and twenty-five would enlist for three months of civilian service, which would require "basic civil defense training." (26)

In a 2006 interview with *New York Daily News* reporter Ben Smith, Emanuel repeated his intention to compel civilian service. Emanuel offered these assurances: if we are worried about having to do fifty jumping jacks, the answer is yes; and the program will include uniforms and barracks. (27)

Obama proposed extending AmeriCorps and the Peace Corps, as well as requiring middle and high school children to serve fifty hours per year; college students would be have to serve one-hundred hours per year. (28) But not to worry, your children may not actually be forced to serve; the government will simply refuse to issue your youngster's high school diploma as punishment. (29) At the time of this writing, the GIVE Act has passed Congress, though House committee staff are insisting that the act will not change the voluntary nature of service at this time.

> In the years after the war I have often asked myself what difference it might have made had I known six million Jews had been annihilated. Before the defeat of Germany and in my frame of unquestioning obedience, it would have made no difference to my loyalty." (30)

Uncle Joe

"Uncle Joe Stalin murdered more people than Hitler"

-Jonah Goldberg

All throughout the 2008 presidential campaign the term "cult of personality" was bandied about. It is a term of derision, but it didn't originate with Obama. Former Soviet premier Nikta Khrushchev used the term to describe the adoration of the masses for murderous dictator Joseph Stalin. Former leader of the USSR Joe Stalin saw fit to eliminate millions of "surplus" people and wipe out the life savings of an entire population. (31)

Westerners had a difficult time grasping the magnitude of Stalin's reign of terror; we had no frame of reference for the concept of Stalinism: unlimited violence is acceptable in pursuit of some supposedly higher purpose.

Like all tyrants, Stalin was the product of an unhappy childhood. His brutal father drank himself to death and was brought up by an ambitious mother. As with Hitler, we see quest for power to defend against unresolved powerless feelings from childhood.

After the Revolution of 1917, Stalin was already a cabinet member; he was elected to general secretary of the central committee of the party in 1922 and began building his base of support. Stalin was loyal to Lenin and didn't deviate from his policies. Stalin had a knack for eliminating his rivals, not unlike an ambitious young Chicago POL. Stalin had his primary rival, Trotsky, executed in 1940. In the name of unity and creating socialism in one country, Stalin terrorized large segments of the population. The result of purges, forced famines, and labor camps combined took approximately 40 million lives.

As Obama fancies himself alternatively the reincarnation of Abraham Lincoln and Franklin Delano Roosevelt, a closer perusal of FDR's policies is in order. Beyond the disastrous New Deal, a massive expansion of government bureaucracy and spending that extended the length of the Great Depression, FDR's dealings with Stalin are revealing.

FDR referred to murderous tyrant Stalin as Uncle Joe, displaying a profound lack of understanding of the Bolshevik dictatorship. FDR was deluded about the true nature of life in the Soviet Union, probably due to a combination of wishful thinking and naiveté. (32)

CIA reports disclose that FDR was so willing to curry favor with Stalin that he abandoned protocol and stayed in Soviet headquarters in Teheran and at Yalta, which enabled Stalin to have him bugged. FDR's policy toward the vicious dictator was to beg, plead and cajole him into cooperation. (33)

FDR believed that his personal charisma was quite sufficient to win over the monstrous Stalin. Such was the arrogance of FDR. Stalin promised FDR that after WWII, he would grant freedom of religion to his people—private ownership of property and greater democracy. Stalin ended up with Poland.

FDR's poor judgment has been blamed on his failing health, specifically clinical depression. CIA reports dispute this theory, as others did not observe symptoms at that time. (34)

Astoundingly, Stalin's poll numbers remain high among the Russian population. The *Chicago Tribune* has reported Stalin's approval ratings in 2006 were nearly 50 percent. (35) The mythology around Stalin persists, as does his socialist legacy, including a perpetual lack of reliable moral standards and a high tolerance for government corruption, as well as a lack of respect for individual human life. (36) Today, Stalin is posthumously enjoying something of an image makeover. New textbooks are emphasizing Stalin's undisputed administrative skills and teaching youngsters that Stalin was forced to use "extreme measures" to turn his nation into a superpower. (37)

Note the similarities between FDR's approach to dealing with Stalin and Obama's stated agenda for dealing with murderous Islamofascists. Thus far, President Obama is mimicking FDR's abysmal lack of judgment and naiveté in his efforts at conciliation with the most dangerous dictators on the planet.

Miscellaneous Murderous Cult Leaders

Although cults and mass movements can take an infinite variety of shapes and sizes, all cult leaders, tyrants, and dictator share common traits. Childhood trauma appears to be part of the cluster, as does malignant narcissism. The ubiquitous trait of personal charisma is also required.

Chief loon of the Branch Davidians, David Koresh, was abandoned by his mother and left with his grandmother at age four, after living with his mother's boyfriend, a violent alcoholic. His mother did eventually resurface and remarry.

Jim Jones, of the Jonestown massacre fame, had "messiah" printed on his business card. He was also a devout communist and, like Frank Marshall Davis, was a friend of Paul Robeson. The lifelong Stalin fan was born to a mother who didn't want children; she had planned to follow her own career interests. (38)

Saddam Hussein was, without question, a malignant narcissist. His narcissism was exacerbated by paranoia. He, like all tyrants, recognized the right confluence of external events and saw the opportunity to seize power. It should be no surprise that Hussein's childhood was not a happy one. His mother tried to abort him and kill herself; she refused to bond with him when he was an infant. Saddam went to live with his maternal uncle, only to be returned to his mother at age three; she abused him psychologically and physically.

Many people suffer from terrible childhoods without growing up to be dangerous tyrants. It takes the right combination of psychopathology and opportunity to develop into someone who is a genuine menace.

Chapter 13

What's So Bad About Communism Anyway?

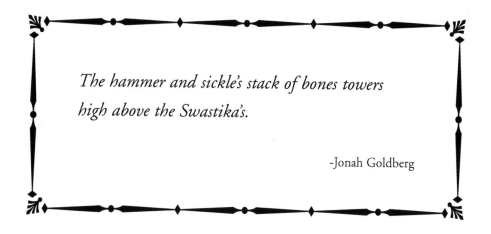

The hammer and sickle's stack of bones towers high above the Swastika's.

-Jonah Goldberg

"Less than 90 minutes after Air Force One landed, the telephone rang. President Obama was on the line wanting to add one more point to a response he had given during an interview with the *New York Times*. On a flight from Ohio to Washington on Friday, Mr. Obama was asked whether

his domestic policies suggested that he is a socialist, as some
conservatives have implied." (1)

Is this a question anyone should have to ask the president of the United States?
Barack Obama told the *New York Times* that "the answer would have to be no."
The president laughed. Recall in deception detection the use of a qualifier like "I
would say the answer is . . ." is common with liars as they attempt to take some
distance from the answer.

Obama was concerned enough to call the reporter and attempt to further explain
himself by blaming former president George W. Bush for increasing the size of
government.

There is nothing in Obama's background to suggest he is anything but a socialist
in the Marxist tradition. His father was a socialist economist, his mother
unabashedly sympathetic to socialist causes. His parents met in a Russian class
when Russia was still the Soviet Union. His most important childhood mentor,
Frank Marshall Davis, was an unapologetic communist and member of the
Communist Party USA. His friends Bill Ayers and Bernardine Dohrn are socialists who advocate the violent overthrow of the United States government. The
"best education of his life" came from Saul Alinsky, yet another socialist. Alinsky
distinguished himself from other revolutionaries of his era by recommending that
the radical learn to blend into the mainstream and played down the use of violence. Obama's bagman, George Soros, is a socialist who despises America.
CPUSA was openly enthusiastic about candidate Obama. (2)

On January 31, 2009, Sam Webb of CPUSA gave a speech extolling the blessings
of the Obama presidency and denouncing capitalism, which, according to Webb,
exists to oppress blacks. Leftists have no sense of irony. Webb also called upon his
fellow travelers to support the Obama administration and called for a new New
Deal, which looked remarkably like Obama's current agenda: close Gitmo and
end torture, pass the Lily Ledbetter Act, increase funding for foreign abortions,
increase fuel efficiency standards, open a dialogue with Arabs and Muslims, send
George Mitchell to the Middle East to push for an independent Palestinian state,
and meet with generals to orchestrate a pullout from Iraq. (3) Candidate Obama

met with and was subsequently endorsed by the Chicago New Party and the Democratic Socialists of America (4).

One of his Chicago mentors, Alice Palmer, was a great admirer of the Soviet Union. Palmer attended the Congress of the Communist Party in the Soviet Union in 1986. Obama expressed his gratitude to Palmer by using legal maneuvering to get her kicked off the ballot when she ran against him for state senate. Palmer decided to run for Congress and asked Obama to be her placeholder in the state senate in case she lost. She did lose and expected her senate seat back. Palmer eventually ran against Obama with the support of Jesse Jackson Jr. Obama hired attorneys to challenge the 1,600 signatures required to get Palmer on the ballot. (5)

Among the elite in the Obama mentor cabal, we also find former Clinton National Security advisor Anthony Lake. Lake was nominated for the position of CIA director but had to withdraw when he told the late journalist Tim Russert that he was unconvinced about Soviet spy Alger Hiss's guilt. (6)

Was there really ever some rational basis to believe that Obama is anything other than a radical socialist?

Credit the public school system for America's apathetic response to Obama's socialist agenda. Pundits are openly asking the question that would not have been asked in generations past: What's so bad about socialism anyway?

Hollywood celebutards have long embraced the most brutal of communist dictators from their lofty Malibu perches. Young people have no frame of reference with which to understand socialism and communism. Obama's youth cult didn't live through the cold war. They don't know about Radio Free Europe, which provided precious information to the victims of communism living behind what was then known as the iron curtain that divided Europe into two areas, making much of Eastern Europe a prison. Armed guards were posted at the borders, and many desperate citizens were killed attempting to flee from a life of oppression.

At one time, Havana, Cuba, was a popular tourist resort. Americans traveled freely to enjoy the nightlife. That all ended when Fidel Castro took over and immediately plundered all private property. Moderates, as well as dissenters, were murdered. Castro ruled his totalitarian communist dictatorship by brute force, driving the nation into poverty, disease, and despair. Human Rights Watch asserts that the government represses nearly all forms of political dissent. Castro's Cuba, now being run by Fidel's brother, Raul, tortures and imprisons its own citizens for daring to speak out against the brutal government.

So harsh is life in Cuba that countless Cubans have lost their lives on tiny boats and rafts desperately trying to get to freedom. We will never know how many Cubans tried to make the ninety-mile trip to Florida seeking the most basic of human rights.

Instinctively, liberals gravitate toward Fidel Castro. He has long been a darling of the celebutard community. These simpletons make trip after trip to Cuba and are not bright enough to realize that every facet of their visit is carefully coordinated to create the illusion of a happy, prosperous nation. One would think that movie actors have enough familiarity with Hollywood sets to catch on. Then again, celebutards are not celebrated for their sagacity.

All communist dictators have played the same game with visiting useful idiots. Mao's government treated celebutards, including Shirley MacLaine, to a highly produced, well-scripted, useful idiot propaganda tours.

Such inanity is to be expected from Hollywood. When the president of the United States embraces the brutal Cuban government, it is cause for apprehension. Barack Obama makes no secret of his longing to establish friendly relations with the Cuban despot.

At the same time, Obama rebuffs the current government of Colombia in its efforts to trade with the United States. Such an arrangement would be beneficial to the United States by providing a buttress against deranged communist dictator Hugo Chavez. Chavez is, predictably, another pet of the Hollywood imbecile community. Colombia's current president, Alvaro Uribe, deserves American support for his efforts to stand up to the Revolutionary Armed Forces of Colombia (FARC), as well as to the drug lords who had been terrorizing the citizenry unchecked for years. Obama's attorney general, Eric Holder, is quite savvy about the narco-terrorist organization. Holder represented Chiquita Banana and was able to negotiate a very favorable settlement with the government for Chiquita, which had been funding another terrorist group in Colombia, the AUC. Between 1997 and 2004, Chiquita gave the AUC nearly two million dollars, ostensibly to pay for protection. To suggest that the Obama administration is not aware of what is going on in Colombia is an affront.

Attorney General Holder has long been kindly disposed toward terrorists. As deputy attorney general in the Clinton administration, he succeeded in squelching lucid voices, including the FBI, who opposed Bill Clinton's pardon of the vicious and bloodthirsty Puerto Rican FALN terrorists.

America's youth have never faced life under tyranny or terrorism; there has always been enough: enough food, enough money, enough stuff. Our left wing schools are not educating students about the reality of the socialist utopias that have consistently failed while making life a living hell for its victims, but providing plenty of perks and power to a small ruling class.

On paper, it sounds swell to the naïve and unsophisticated; spread the wealth, as candidate Obama explained to Joe the Plumber. Level the playing field; the government will take care of everything. Free health care. No big bonuses for Wall Street fat cats. What could be better?

As with all mass movements, there is little genuine ideological sincerity in the movement. Recruitment is the goal and it is best achieved by seizing on times of failure and frustration within the populace. Hope is the main reason people are swayed by mass movements. Obama made false hope the centerpiece of his fraudulent campaign.

In a socialist state, the government owns the means of production. This means government control of businesses, as well as the distribution of goods and services. If you are delighted with your mail service and admire the smooth efficiency with which the government runs Medicare, socialism might be for you. The ultimate goal of a socialist fantasy would be social justice, that amorphous, nice-sounding non-concept.

The various definitions of socialism are necessarily vague; it's a theory that has never worked. It fails because it runs contrary to basic human nature. For all of the lofty-sounding ivory-tower rhetoric about working together for the common good, humans are not wired that way.

Americans are the most generous people on earth; show us a natural disaster, and we can't whip our checkbooks out quickly enough. We overload online servers trying to get our donations in. Note: this is true only of *normal* Americans. Liberals, Obama included, are notoriously stingy when it comes to charitable giving when it involves their own money.

What people resent is being forced to give up their hard-earned income to support those who choose not to participate in what we refer to as work. Socialism mandates surrendering enormous control over our lives to a powerful centralized government in the absurd belief that they will act in our best interests. When has that ever happened?

History is rife with examples of the failures of socialism. Hitler's Nazi Party was socialist; remember his was the National *Socialist* German Workers' Party. We know how that turned out. Or ask the happy and well fed citizens of Cuba how that socialism thing is working out for them. Cubans risk their lives on rafts and boats trying to escape this grand social experiment. The ideology has failed in the USSR, China, and Eastern Europe. Western Europe has experimented with "democratic socialism," and it has been a disaster. So calamitous has European socialism been that European Union leaders have warned Obama against following the same toxic policies.

Jeffrey Folks writes about his time in Yugoslavia in the 1980s:

> Anyone who has lived inside the demoralized, unproductive, gray prison of a communist state, as I did in the mid-1980s knows to what depths of impoverishment the egalitarian fantasies of socialism inevitably lead. They lead to decades of

frustrated poverty and lifetimes of untreated illness culminating in early death. I remember the columns of death notices for men and women in their forties and fifties that appeared in the local newspaper. Gradually I learned to associate those death notices with the lack of fresh foodstuffs, the travesty of state health care, and the pervasive demoralization of an enslaved population drowning itself in cheap alcohol and cigarettes. (7)

Socialism creates "pervasive demoralization" by removing incentives. Why bother to get an education or work hard if your income will be confiscated by the state and redistributed to whomever the government sees fit? Most of us don't want to work just to subsidize those who are too lazy and unproductive to earn their own income.

Thus, the spirit of the brightest, most ambitious, and most talented is crushed. Meanwhile, the power elites in government sacrifice nothing and enjoy outrageous perks at our expense, not unlike House Speaker Nancy Pelosi's abuse of a military jet.

Liberals have been trying to sell us on socialism for decades; they have created and elevated an imaginary victim class: the poor, single moms, the disenfranchised whatever label they think we will buy. Expanding a centralized government and redistributing your income, according to the Left, is the only way these lost souls can experience fairness.

Never mind the fact that a free market system has allowed even the lowest earners in the nation to enjoy a lifestyle that is the envy of millions of real poor people throughout the world. Our poor have color TVs, air conditioning, and enough food.

Socialism is the bridge between capitalism and communism. In a communist state, all private property rights are abolished. To strip citizens of their property rights requires that the government use *force*. Throughout history, we have seen murderous thugs: Hitler, Stalin, Pol Pot, Chavez, Castro, and others use force against their own citizens to seize and maintain power. Millions of innocent citizens have been slaughtered in the name of creating a socialist utopia. We don't need guards at our borders to keep people *in*.

You will note that Obama, like all socialists, makes a lot of racket about "the poor" and the "workers." We are supposed to believe that allowing the government to grab maximum power is going to help the working class. They always say that. But in actual practice, socialism is cherished only by intellectuals and benefits only the elites, not the workers.

By strengthening the labor unions, the central government can use them in its push to nationalize and take over private industry.

Like his favorite teacher, Saul Alinsky, Obama is a fan of Marxism, another failed socialist ideology. Marxists view labor as a commodity that is valued by the cost of production. In other words, anything produced is worth only the actual cost of production. To seek a profit over and above the actual cost of production is wrong under a Marxist system. Marx called for revolution and believed the shortest route to utopia was the abolition of private property.

It's as absurd as it sounds. Marxists invariably offer up the same bait; socialism will prevent the inevitable boom and bust cycles associated with capitalism. Sound familiar? Current Treasury Secretary Tim Geithner has been repeating that mantra for weeks as justification for a massive power grab by the executive branch.

Boom and bust cycles are natural and necessary in a free market system. Incentives like wages and the lack of oppressive regulation lead to a high degree of productivity. In time, this productivity will lead to an excess of goods in the marketplace, driving prices down. If the government stays out of it, the market will naturally right itself quickly again by pulling back on production. When practiced as a true free market system, capitalism is as close to failure proof as we can get. It works because it is harmonious with human nature. A free market system leads to creativity and innovation. American capitalism has created a standard of living the rest of the world can only dream of. Our free market system has uplifted millions in our country and those truly suffering throughout the world. No system has provided so many opportunities for so many. It's a personal choice what you do with that freedom. It is not a perfect system; we are flawed beings. But it beats any other system by an infinite margin. Radicals like Obama who trash America and her free market system seek only to seize power at the expense of the very people they pretend to want to help. If the Left really wanted to help the poor, they would get off the backs of small business, the country's largest source of employment; eliminate heavy-handed regulation and confiscatory taxation, which as sure as night will turn into day, will lead to more and better-paying jobs.

Communism is the end game for the socialist. Under communist rule, all private property rights have been abolished, and the state has absolute control over every aspect of the citizen's life. There is much intellectual debate about the differences between communism and socialism. In common parlance, the differences are negligible, though communism is often distinguished from socialism by virtue of the communist government's zeal in using force against its own citizens.

The Obama administration is pushing his socialist agenda, using what the Left refers erroneously to as the failure of capitalism.

We are not witnessing the failure of capitalism. We are not a true capitalist economy. For years, we have been allowing big government and big business to blur their boundaries until we now have an economic system closer to Benito Mussolini's corporate statism than true capitalism. In an ideal capitalistic society, all means of production are privately owned and operated. Corporate America and big government are now thoroughly enmeshed. As is typical, when big government got involved in corporate America, corporate America was corrupted. The federal government has been encroaching on private enterprise with evermore increasing regulations and burdens. Witness the waddling back and forth that goes on between the public and private sector. The same players keep turning up on both sides of the same fence. One day you're a bureaucrat in charge of harassing executives. The next day, you're in someone's cabinet, only to return to the private sector another day. Big business hates risk. Getting cozy with politicians is one way of reducing risk; this is why so much Wall Street money makes its way into political campaigns. Obama raked in enormous sums from big businesses, yet the mythology persists that Wall Street is run by greedy, cigar-smoking Republicans.

As predictable as daylight, increasing government interference assured the disruption of our economic system. We can track in a straight line the collapse of the housing industry right back to the Community Reinvestment Act (CRA), which was created during the happy and prosperous Carter years, creating a shakedown mandate for corrupt community organizations like ACORN. At taxpayer expense, groups like ACORN were able to literally force banks to make loans to borrowers who would not be able to repay them. In 1999, under pressure from the Clinton administration, Fannie Mae further relaxed credit requirements for subprime borrowers and generated staggering profits for itself and such luminaries as Jamie Gorelick and Franklin Raines.

Fannie Mae is itself an example of a Mussolini-style economic unit. Fannie is some sort of monstrous government/private sector hybrid. This kind of ill-conceived breeding program keeps spawning bigger, more corrupt, and more inept agencies. There is nothing capitalistic about Fannie Mae or the government-backed mortgage system.

Obama and the rest of the Left are taking advantage of the collective economic ignorance of the population by insisting that the economic meltdown was caused by capitalism run amok. Without strict government controls, we are supposed to believe capitalistic greed will devour the universe. Why are people buying this?

The other issue America is ignoring at her peril is the conduct of the government using its power to harass private citizens. This didn't start with the much-maligned AIG, but emboldened by the new administration. Congress has taken its boundary-violating to unprecedented levels. The asinine baseball hearings were bad enough. What we are seeing today is genuine abuse of power. Not content to simply harass and demonize the employees at AIG, they are now busying themselves trying to pass draconian ex post facto legislation targeting the executive bonuses.

Can thinking people set aside, for a moment, the schadenfreude of it all, and consider the real implications of this type of persecution of private citizens by our highest elected officials? Keeping in mind that socialism is a tough sell to people who actually know what it is, it is no surprise that the current liberal Congress is preparing for assaults in free speech, including attempting to reintroduce the absurdly named Fairness Doctrine. Which, by the way, will be done by way of bureaucratic regulations, rather than legislation, which would at least expose it to the light of day.

Socialism fails because it is so out of synch with human nature. It robs people of their God-given right to liberty. For all of the utopian dogma, it is simply not the nature of humans to sacrifice their labors for a common good. It certainly is the antithesis of what our Founding Fathers had in mind. They drafted our divinely inspired Constitution for the sole purpose of *restraining* the power of a centralized government. Too many Americans think the Constitution says our rights come from the government. Our founders were well aware what happens when a central government gets too much power; they fought a long and bloody war to escape that kind of tyranny. The Constitution sets strict limits on what the federal government can legitimately do, and the rights of the federal government are pretty minimal. Activist judges have consistently overreached and expanded the power of the federal government in ways that are directly in conflict with our Constitution. It's excruciatingly clear that Obama has no use for our magnificent Constitution.

The most iniquitous facet of socialism is moral relativism. There is no right or wrong for the socialist. Saul Alinsky taught that the end justifies the means. The state replaces other institutions including family and church as the source of all sustenance. This kind of moral nihilism enables heinous acts: the holocaust, Stalinism, Pol Pot's killing fields, and the murderous regimes of Castro and Hugo Chavez. Liberals like to delude themselves that the reason socialism has failed with such noteworthy consistency is because nobody has yet practiced it perfectly. If only, they wail, they could just get a whack at implementing Marxism in the United States, they promise it would work this time, something Marx himself failed to accomplish.

This lack of moral consistency inevitably leads to corruption: businesses pay protection money, government officials ignore internal corruption, and improperly vetting the country's leaders becomes unobjectionable. (8) Machiavelli taught that the rejection of moral standards is a tactical necessity for the charismatic redeemer. (9)

The sine qua non of communism is the diminution in value of individual human life. The collective is all; the state replaces God as the state must be completely separate from any notion of a power greater than itself. This lack of value on life is prominent in the liberal pro-choice platform. Obama has shown himself to be far more radical on the life issue than even such stalwart liberal hacks as Barbara Boxer (D-California). Obama not only supports partial birth abortion, he would deny treatment to infants born alive following botched abortions. He is entirely comfortable with allowing an innocent baby to perish in a linen closet a few hours after birth. In a socialist society, humans become expendable; oppressed humans don't value their own lives or the lives of others the way a free population does. As we hurtle toward socialized medicine, it's worth considering that less effort will be devoted to providing treatment for the critically ill, and less effort will be directed toward preventing unnatural deaths in a culture that has ceased to cherish individual life.

As president, Obama wasted no time in announcing his plan to reverse the Provider Refusal Rule, which expanded a thirty-year-old law establishing a "conscience clause" for health care workers who do not want to participate in abortions.

Valiant American citizen Captain Richard Phillips, who commanded the US merchant vessel, the *Maersk Alabama*, was held captive by Somali pirates. Fox News host Geraldo Rivera moderated a debate between conservative author Ann Coulter and liberal pundit Kirsten Powers. Coulter was outraged at the Obama administration's failure to take swift action to free Captain Phillips. Powers perfectly synopsized the Left's arrant disregard for individual life. Powers castigated Coulter and those who were making too big of a deal about "just one American hostage." This is a perfect example of the socialist concept that human life is expendable.

The Communist Manifesto

Karl Marx set forth the ten planks of The *Communist Manifesto* as the test to determine whether a society had truly achieved communism. Technically, we must credit Karl Marx in 1848, not the current Democratic Party, for the ten planks, though the similarities are conspicuous: (10)

1. Abolition of private property and the application of all rents of land to public purposes.

2. A heavy progressive or graduated income tax.

3. Abolition of all right of inheritance.

4. Confiscation of the property of all emigrants and rebels.

5. Centralization of credit in the hands of the state, by means of a national bank with State capital and an exclusive monopoly.

6. Centralization of the means of communications and transport in the hands of the State.

7. Extension of factories and instruments of production owned by the state, the bringing into cultivation of wastelands, and the improvement of the soil generally in accordance with a common plan.

8. Equal liability of all to labor. Establishment of industrial armies, especially for agriculture.

9. Combination of agriculture with manufacturing industries, gradual abolition of the distinction between town and country, by a more equitable distribution of population over the country.

10. Free education for all children in public schools, Abolition of children's factory labor in its present form. Combination of education with industrial production.

Platform of the Communist Party USA (CPUSA)

Today, the CPUSA has adopted a refurbished set of planks: (11)

1. Immediate relief
   1.1 A moratorium on foreclosures and evictions.
   1.2 Reset mortgages so payments are affordable.
   1.3 No bailouts for banks.
   1.4 Extend unemployment compensation, increase payments and eligibility.
   1.5 Increase food stamps, WIC, children's health insurance, low-income energy assistance.
   1.6 Assist state and local governments.

    1.7   Fund ready-to-go infrastructure projects.

2. A Peacetime, Green Jobs Economy for All
   - 2.1   Enact massive public works.
   - 2.2   Make existing buildings energy efficient.
   - 2.3   Construct new schools, affordable housing, mass transit and bridges.
   - 2.4   Major clean, affordable energy development projects for solar, wind, and biomass.
   - 2.5   Program to cut greenhouse gas emissions, environmental cleanup.
   - 2.6   Restore energy regulation and public ownership of utilities.
   - 2.7   Enact the Employee Free Choice Act.
   - 2.8   Enact HR 676, US National Health Insurance Act, single payer.
   - 2.9   Fund public education, pre-school through higher and technical
   - 2.10 No privatization of Social Security or Medicare
   - 2.11 Expand and improve Social Security and Medicare Benefits.

3. Restore Civil Rights, Bill of Rights, Separation of Powers
   - 3.1   Restore Civil Rights Act enforcement, affirmative action.
   - 3.2   Outlaw hate crimes.
   - 3.3   *Preserve Roe v. Wade.*
   - 3.4   Immigration reform with path to citizenship, no militarization of borders.
   - 3.5   No exploitive guest worker programs.
   - 3.6   No human being is illegal.
   - 3.7   Repeal the Patriot Act.
   - 3.8   Investigate and prosecute Bush administration violations.
   - 3.9   Expand voting rights.
   - 3.10 Enact publicly financed elections.
   - 3.11 Same-day registration.
   - 3.12 Voting rights for ex-felons.
   - 3.13 Restore Fairness Doctrine in media.

4. Strength Through Peace
   - 4.1   Withdraw US troops from Iraq with no bases or US corporations left behind.

4.2   Full care for returning veterans.

4.3   No war on Iran.

4.4   No expansion of troops in Afghanistan.

4.5   Assistance in Iraq to rebuild Iraq.

4.6   New foreign policy of diplomacy, respect for all nations.

4.7   Renew commitment to UN.

4.8   End trade policies that enrich corporations and destroy jobs.

4.9   Ratify Kyoto Treaty and other climate change agreements.

4.10   Enforce nuclear non-proliferation.

4.11   Work to abolish nuclear weapons.

4.12   Cut Pentagon spending in half.

4.13   Close down US bases around the world.

With only a few exceptions, Obama has performed magnificently according to the CPUSA. His sending of additional troops into Afghanistan represents a desertion of plank 4.4, although communists can console themselves with Obama's slashing of defense spending and his sending of half the number of troops requested by the generals in command. Pundits seem to think Obama is ramping up our presence in Afghanistan in hopes of preventing another attack on American soil, which would be considered a negative by many Americans at reelection time. That may well be his impetus. But also contemplate what America was like immediately after 9/11. We went through a wave of unprecedented patriotism. At the same time, Americans were united in our desire to take the fight to our enemies. Obama would be served well by neither a surge in patriotism nor a rejuvenation of our will to defend ourselves.

As Randall Hoven astutely observes, whoever wrote the first stimulus bill must have had CPUSAs list handy. (12) Leftists are always lacking in imagination; perchance the feeble-minded Nancy Pelosi has learned how to copy and paste.

The CPUSA no longer endorses candidates for president. But they did not attempt to hide their enchantment with Obama

Divide and Conquer

Never known for originality, the left ran in 2008 on the quotidian divide and conquer program. Liberals relish assigning humans to groups which they then anoint with special victim status for the purpose of being used in their destructive power schemes. Liberals are obsessed with race. It harkens back to the old Soviet Union days in which blacks were openly recruited as operatives by the Kremlin to be exploited in the cause of destabilizing American democracy. Leftist policies will never be accepted by free people if the people know what they are. Liberals can only get their agenda through if they induce discord and chaos among the populace.

Race and class warfare are liberal contrivances. As Obama and the Pelosi/Reid cabal attempt to ram socialism down the collective American throat, note the anti-success, anti-capitalist bombast. Obama would have you believe that successful people can only achieve success by plundering the less prosperous. This is the grand deception upon which all forms of collectivism balance.

Every single time Obama-style income redistribution policies are tried, they fail. Not only do these kinds of oppressive schemes fail to raise the overall standard of living for the population, they kill happiness.

Economic freedom is an essential element in national happiness. Freedom causes happiness. Liberals tell us that a free market economy causes misery and we would all be happier without the vagaries of capitalism. Like all liberal economic theories, the reverse is true. The freer the economy, the happier the population (13).

Under the Soviet ministry known as Gosplan, economic planning was hijacked by central planning to control supply and demand. The result was unmitigated disaster, creating massive shortages and surpluses leading to a near economic collapse by the 1960's (14).

Hence, Obama's embrace of exactly the same calamitous policies. The most rudimentary review of history provides more than enough unambiguous proof that collectivism simply does not work. If it did, millions of innocent lives would not have been taken to prevent citizens from seeking freedom; armed guards would not be executing those who would risk all to escape oppressive governments in Cuba and Iran.

The Left's phantasmagorical foolishness about leveling the playing field will not only bankrupt us and lower our standard of living, it will make us, collectively, miserable. The same policies that are tolerable to Europeans will be anathema to free-spirited Americans.

"But one recent study goes even further and asserts that Americans differ *genetically* from people in most other countries. A simple version of the argument starts with the observation that immigrants tend to be entrepreneurial, willing to give up security and familiarity for the possibility of prosperity and success. This trait is relatively rare-a mutation from the norm. Very few people in Old World communities had it, and those who did were more likely to migrate from their homeland than those who did not. But because America is quite literally a nation of immigrants-or descendants of immigrants-and these immigrants (or their descendants) have married other immigrants (or their descendants), the genetic mutation that leads to entrepreneurial behavior appears with unusual frequency in our citizens. According to this line of argument, America's vast success can be explained by our genetic predisposition to embrace risk with potentially explosive rewards." (15)

Americans are different, dare we say *exceptional*. It has taken an extraordinary amount of deceit and manipulation over decades to bring America to the brink of accepting Obama style of overbearing governance.

For all the liberal caterwauling about exploitation by the evil rich in America, the reality is that Americans are at their happiest when they are working. We are not necessarily working simply to accumulate wealth; one of our distinctly American traits is our ability to derive genuine joy out of the creation of value irrespective of the financial worth attached to our labor. Naturally, most Americans want to earn good wages but our inner happiness is pegged to our sense of accomplishment in the creation of value, not to an arbitrary number. (16)

One of the many ways in which Obama is pursuing his manifesto of assured universal despair is by aiming for massive unemployment. Over taxation and burdensome regulation drives employers to reduce staff, go out of business or relocate out of the country. Liberals see these as positive outcomes. If the private sector is debilitated by the government, the people will be compelled to depend more on government for their elemental subsistence.

"Involuntary unemployment is a disaster for happiness because-beyond the economic misfortune it creates-it strips away the sense of control people need in their lives." (17) The only thing that could make you more miserable than being unemployed would be receiving "help" from your government. Receiving government assistance seems to have an especially deleterious impact on individual happiness. No other single factor has been found to account for predicting unhappiness as reliably as government assistance. (18)

Government assistance has an instant impact on the individual psyche. Over the longer term, the stage is set for what psychologists call learned helplessness. Research psychologist Martin Seligman accidentally discovered the relationship between learned helplessness and depression. Seligman found that people develop the symptoms of depression when they feel as if they lack sufficient control over their lives. Obama's policies represent a singularly efficacious mechanism for inducing collective national depression.

Americans do not become depressed due to perceived inequalities in income distribution. We are quite happy with our lots in life provided we have a sense of the possibility of upward mobility. Being poor at this moment does not create misery. A belief that we have no ability to change our circumstances is what creates lifelong despair. An over-controlling government is by far, the most potent purveyor of gross national misery.

Economists have studied the impact of government spending on public happiness and found that as government grows, the percentage of the population that is satisfied with life shrinks. (19)

The more government does, the less happy we become. People look around and become frustrated with government pork and wasteful spending. Resentment over excessive taxation builds. And as regulation becomes ever more burdensome, while accomplishing little of benefit, the inevitable rise in unemployment fuels learned helplessness leading to a cycle of increasing depression and dependency that is distinctly un-American.

Agenda for Amerika

Yuri Alexandrovic Bezmenov defected from the Soviet Union to the West in 1970. He escaped at great risk to his life to get away from the collective system so revered by liberals and celebutards. After a long career in the Soviet press, Bezmenov calls us out on our complacency as the United States government follows the old Soviet model of ideological subversion inching toward the George Soros hoax of a New World Order. Our enemies in Russia invest a mere fifteen-percent of their time, money and resources into espionage; the greater threat to our freedom comes from what Bezmenov calls ideological subversion; a slow brainwashing process in four stages. (20)

The first stage is demoralization, a process which requires fifteen to twenty years to accomplish; the amount of time necessary to educate one generation of students to the doctrine of your enemy. Ayers-based education has clearly hit its target.

> "In other words, Marxism-Leninism ideology is being pumped into the soft heads of at least 3 generation of American students without being challenged or counterbalanced by the basic values of Americanism; American patriotism." (21)

But merely preaching to the choir, spouting Marxism at leftwing universities does not produce the desired outcomes. The KGB had to get its ideology into our mainstream. Hollywood celebutards, politicians and other useful idiots are actually entirely expendable.

> "Try to get into, large circulation, established conservative media. Reach filthy rich movie makers, intellectuals in so-

called academic circles. Cynical, ego-centric people who can
look into your eyes with angelic expression and tell you a lie.
This are the most recruitable people; people who lack moral
principals - who are either too greedy or too, uh, suffer from
self-importance, uh, they feel that they matter a lot. Uh, these
are the people who KGB wanted very much to recruit." (22)

Those idiots are only useful until the destabilization of the culture is complete.

"So basically America is stuck, with demoralization; and
unless, even if you start right now this minute; you start
educating new generation of Americans - it will still take you
15 to 20 years to turn the tide of uh, ideological perception of
reality; back to normalcy and patriotism.

The result? The result you can see -- most of the people who graduated in the 60s,
dropouts or half-baked intellectuals, are now occupying the positions of power in
the government, civil service, business, mass media, and educational systems. You
are stuck with them.

You can't get rid of to them. They are contaminated. They are
programmed to think and react to certain stimuli in a certain
pattern [alluding to Pavlov]. You cannot change their mind
even if you expose them to authentic information." (23)

The demoralization of America is, according to Bezmenov, complete. The putre-
fcation of our pop culture affected exactly the kind of dissolution in moral order
that the One Worlder's need to achieve hegemony.

The government has to promise all manner of goodies and freebies to move the
populace against the free market system. A free and open competitive market is
too strong of a bulwark against the New World Order agenda.

The next essential phase, destabilization is brief, requiring only two to five years
to complete. The essentials are at the forefront: the economy, foreign relations

and defense. Bezmenov sees Marxist-Leninist influence throughout each of the essential sectors.

After the destabilization phase comes inevitable crisis. Bezmenov warns that it can take as little as six weeks to bring a country to the verge of crisis. Team Obama operates in perpetual crisis invention mode, drawing expertly from the New World Order playbook as outlined by Bezmenov.

The purpose of the crisis is, as Rahm Emanuel has observed, to create opportunities for corrupt politicians to enhance their dominion. After an upheaval, which may include violence, the nation enjoys a sense of "normalization" which is an artificial sense of stability brought about by the artificial crises that preceded it.

Perhaps the words of Bezmenov explain how Alaska Governor Sarah Palin has captured the hearts of so many conservatives. Patriotic Americans are intuitively drawn to her natural sunny and relentless patriotism as the counter weight to the gloomy negativity being promulgated by the left.

Obama is and always has been a socialist and a Soros globalist; he scarcely knows any other dogma. He is forcing the United States into socialism at dangerous velocity. Leaders in the European Union are issuing admonitions about Obama's socialist policies. Trust them; they know.

Chapter 14

An Un-American President

Less than six months into it and the Barack Hussein Obama presidency has been unmitigated mayhem. Obama- caused disasters befall the nation on a near daily basis, one can scarcely keep track anymore. We have endured his offensive schmoozing with the slave owners' tour in the Arab states, punctuated by his contemptible speech in Cairo, in which the president spouted flagrant falsehoods about the charms of Islam, while berating the United States for being a bit churlish about radical Muslim ideology after 9/11. As anticipated, Obama made apocryphal pledges to Muslims about the United States' ability to constrain Israel.

Six months into the presidency of Obama and doubts still remain as to his eligibility to serve as Commander in Chief. Our Founding Fathers set forth basic requirements for the presidency by way of Article II, Section 1 of the United States Constitution:

> No person except a natural born citizen, or a citizen of the United States, at the time of the adoption of this Constitution, shall be eligible to the office of President; neither shall any person be eligible to that office who shall not have attained to the age of thirty five years, and been fourteen years a resident within the United States.

To date, Obama has resisted all demands that he produce acceptable documentation of these most elementary requirements. Common sense dictates that Obama's willingness to spend hundreds of thousands of dollars in legal fees rather than produce a valid birth certificate should give us pause.

Our Founders put nothing in the Constitution about vetting a future president, leaving that serious task to the people.

The most slapdash review makes it manifestly clear that Obama would have been subject to considerable scrutiny if he were required to apply for the most basic security clearance. Obama's mysterious past, experiences abroad, and nihilistic friends would have mandated more than a casual review of his application.

In actuality, nobody vetted Obama. We should have known the DNC wouldn't. Relying on the DNC to vet a candidate would be as derelict as putting Geithner in charge of the IRS. The American people were obliged to do the vetting. We are supposed to have a non-partisan, autonomous press just for this kind of thing. Instead, the fourth estate collapsed completely into a propaganda arm for the Democrat party.

We have always been able to boast that in America, anyone can grow up to be president. Ostensibly, that includes America hating radicals who pose a grave threat to our national security. I'm not sure this is precisely what our Founding Fathers had in mind.

A few lawsuits demanding the production of relevant documents are gaining some traction in the courts. With the nation currently under a one party rule, it is not clear how the issue will ultimately resolve. Nowhere is the power of cultism more apparent than when we reflect on how easily the public was persuaded to hand over the keys to the White House to a complete stranger who may not even be an American.

Marginally American Presidents

The job of the United States President is to represent the interests in the United States. Even terrible presidents have historically understood this. All presidents will, at times, take actions counter to our national interest. Barack Obama is the first who openly chooses to act to undermine the United States.

Pre- Obama, Jimmy Carter has long been reviled as the worst president in American history. Carter's bungling of the presidency was more than his manifest inadequacy. Carter brazenly supported America's most dangerous enemies, enabling the rise of the Islamofacist thugocracy in Iran. Islamic terrorism, including 9/11 can be tracked back in a straight line back to Carter.

"For many years, Iran has defined itself in part by its opposition to my country, and there is in fact a tumultuous history between us. In the middle of the Cold War, the United States played a role in the overthrow of a democratically elected Iranian government. "

Of all the opprobrious anti- American twaddle spewed by Obama in his much-exalted Cairo speech, this statement may be one of the most malignant. Obama essentially apologized for what was a colossal CIA success: the removal of Mohammad Mossadegh from power in Iran. The mission, known as Operation Ajax, was supported by President Dwight Eisenhower and Winston Churchill. Mossadegh was a crackpot, which is why the Left finds him so compelling. Churchill described Mossadegh as "an elderly lunatic bent on wrecking his country and handing it over to the Communists." (1)

Mossadegh's platform was his fierce opposition to British influence, an ideology adopted by Obama. Paving the way for future deranged dictators, Mossadegh eventually fired the parliament, called for a special election and declared himself the winner of ninety-nine percent of the vote.

Mossadegh nationalized the oil wells. That was ruinous enough, but batty Mohammad ostensibly didn't realize that once the Brits pulled out of Iran, there was nobody who actually knew how to run them. Thus, he drove his people into abject destitution. The West had well founded jitters about Iran's economic plight making the country easy prey for the Soviet Union.

After the CIA orchestrated coup, the former Shah, Mohammad Reza Pahlavi, returned from exile and modernized the country, including granting women the right to vote, raising the hackles of Muslim extremists. The gains made for women were systematically reversed when Khomeini seized power.

The Shah was a friend of the United States. Indeed, he was a flawed leader, prone to despotism but a real pussycat compared to the current Iranian thugocracy. Until former president Jimmy Carter took office, the United States and Iran maintained a stable relationship. Carter couldn't abandon the Shah fast enough. The daffy left always gets hysterical about minor despots and glorifies the really barbaric ones. Fidel Castro is a demigod to a libtard. Carter's refusal to support the Shah and his delusions about the Ayatollah Khomeini enabled the savage fanatical regime to grab control of Iran. Khomeini's government slaughtered more citizens in its first few weeks than the Shah's regime killed during its entire thirty-eight year reign. The incendiary ayatollah's take over was the beginning of the worldwide eruption of Islamic terrorism.

Indeed, Carter has been a real trailblazer in becoming the worst former president in history. The peanut farmer continues unabated in his assaults on the United States and Israel via his never ending canoodling with terrorists dedicated to our annihilation.

Carter, however, is an American. We know where he was born. We know he served in the military. Carter grew up with the same traditions and values as the rest of America in most fundamental ways.

Hail to the Thief

Barack Obama is profoundly beholden to the Clintons. Bill Clinton made anti-Americanism tolerable. Former president Clinton was animated by avariciousness rather than an irresistible compulsion to extirpate the republic, but he lowered the bar dramatically as to the qualities we require in our leaders.

Draft dodger Clinton made no real secret of his antipathy toward our military and his political beliefs are nothing more than warmed over hippie slop.

"When Bill Clinton took office in 1993, China presented no threat to the United States. Chinese missiles 'couldn't hit the side of a barn,'" notes Timothy W. Maier of Insight Magazine. Few could reach North America and those that made it would likely miss their targets.

"Thanks to Clinton, China can now hit any city in the USA, using state-of-the-art solid-fueled missiles with dead-accurate, computerized guidance systems and multiple warheads.

China probably has suitcase nukes as well. These enable China to strike by proxy equipping nuclear-armed terrorists to do its dirty work while the Chinese play innocent. Some intelligence sources claim that China maintains secret stockpiles of chemical, biological and nuclear weapons on U.S. soil, for just such contingencies." (2)

The reason for China's sudden rapid development of military technology? Bill Clinton sold it to them. Some secrets were simply given away via declassification. Nobody in history has done as much to provide hi-tech arms for China.

Clinton's efforts to cover up his connections with Communist China led to the employment of the ignoble Jamie Gorelick to the Justice Department. Gorelick's role in bringing about 9/11 was conspicuous. Focused on covering up Clinton's traitorous dealings with China, Gorelick erected the now exposed barrier between the FBI and CIA, effectively neutering the intelligence community.

In Clintonland, the loss of innocent American lives was a small price to pay to cover up his unambiguously treasonous conduct with Communist China.

Obama is not the first anti-American president but he is our first truly un-American president.

All of our prior United States presidents have been essentially American, though certainly some more patriotic than others. Obama's connection to America is tenuous at best.

Living in a Lefty Paradise

If we choose to believe that Barack Obama was indeed born in Hawaii, we must recognize that Hawaii in the 1960's was not a place infused with traditional

American values. The state had just been admitted to the union and represented a novel and exotic paradise rich with its own traditions, but lacking a long connection to American history.

Obama seldom talked about his growing up in Hawaii during the campaign signaling he understood the difficulty Middle America would have understanding his background. It was not by coincidence that when Obama decided to get serious about his political future, he became a senator from Illinois, the center of the country.

Hawaii attracted Obama mentor and devout communist, Frank Marshall Davis. In fact, the communist party operated freely in Hawaii, a state lacking in strong cultural ties to the mainland at the time. Hawaii in the 1960's was a Petri dish for America hating communist operatives like Davis and had just suffered through the Honolulu Seven trial of Longshoremen's Union leaders along with other Communist Party members. Davis was intimately involved in the defense of the Honolulu Seven.

Communists controlled the ILWU, the ILWU controlled the Hawaii Democratic Party, and in 1954, union-based election campaigns launched the Hawaii Democrats into control of the legislature. John A. Burns' union-based 1962 capture of the governor's office created a one-party state unbroken for four decades until the election of Republican Governor Linda Lingle in 2002. During those decades in some sessions sat as few as one Republican legislator.

The story of Frank Marshall Davis, Obama's Marxist mentor, is completely intertwined with the story of the Hawaii Democrats rise to power. (3)

What was young Barry taught about American history during his years on the island?

Turning Javanese

At the age other children were learning the Pledge of Allegiance and the story of George Washington's cherry tree, little Barry was in a backwards Third World nation struggling for its very survival. The future president attended Indonesian schools. Presumably, scant attention was given to the study of American history or geography. Obama's mother, Ann unambiguously rejected America in favor of the Javanese lifestyle.

So strong are the ties forged in childhood that the president has referred to Jakarta as his hometown:

> "Oh, I need to come to Indonesia soon. I expect to be traveling to Asia at some point within the next year and I would be surprised if when I came to Asia I did not stop by my old home town of Jakarta. And I'll go visit Menteng Dalam and have some bakso nasi goreng. These are some special dishes here that I used to eat when I was a kid." (4)

While nobody would seriously argue that there is no benefit in a future president having traveled extensively throughout the world, there is little in Obama's history to suggest he has developed an internal sense of himself as American.

Death to the Patriot

The radicals running our public school system have dedicated themselves to extirpating any sense of patriotism in America's children. History has been rewritten, making the United States the perpetual imperialistic, jingoistic villain. Rising anti-Semitism is but one example of the execrable expositions going on in our public schools and universities.

Primed in childhood to believe that the United States is the source of all evil on earth, its small wonder so many young voters felt at ease with a candidate who had so little regard for America and whose story, while entertaining, was hardly the foundation for an appreciation of the greatness of America.

Candidates seeking the presidency typically campaign on a distinctly American platform. Ronald Reagan's unshakable belief in American exceptionalism drove him to seek to make a wonderful nation even better. Other candidates acknowledge America's greatness, but convince us we have lost touch with our better selves and that we need a restoration.

Obama was the first candidate in American history to campaign on a proclamation of "America Sucks."

America, according to Obama, really ought to be thoroughly ashamed of herself. Cultivated by America hating radicals, the current Oval Office Occupant has little to say in America's favor. As his wife, Michelle, told us, our only chance to ever do anything right would be to elect her husband as president.

What is appalling is that this is so un-appalling.

> "I've spoken of the shining city all my political life, but I don't know if I ever quite communicated what I saw when I said it. But in my mind it was a tall, proud city built on rocks stronger than oceans, windswept, God-blessed, and teeming with people of all kinds living in harmony and peace; a city with free ports that hummed with commerce and creativity. And if there had to be city walls, the walls had doors and the doors were open to anyone with the will and heart to get there. That's how I saw it, and see it still." Ronald Wilson Reagan.

> "In other words, the use of patriotism as a political sword or a political shield is as old as the Republic. Still, what is striking about today's patriotism debate is the degree to which it remains rooted in the culture wars of the 1960s in arguments that go back forty years or more. In the early years of the civil rights movement and opposition to the Vietnam War, defenders of the status quo often accused anybody who questioned the wisdom of government policies of being unpatriotic. Meanwhile, some of those in the so-called counter-culture of the Sixties reacted not merely by criticizing particular government policies, but by attacking the symbols, and in extreme cases, the very idea, of America itself by burning flags; by blaming America for all that was wrong with the world; and perhaps most tragically, by failing to honor

those veterans coming home from Vietnam, something that remains a national shame to this day." Barack Hussein Obama.

Don't Know Much About History

Only in a thoroughly dumbed down America would Barack Obama's astonishing ignorance of American history go unnoticed. In his recent agonizing Cairo speech, the president mangled both American and Islamic history:

> "I know that Islam has always been a part of America's story," Mr. Obama told the throng of unenlightened Muslims. "The first nation to recognize my country was Morocco… And since our founding, American Muslims have enriched the United States.
>
> "They [Muslims] have fought in our wars. They have served in our government. They have stood for civil rights. They have started businesses. They have taught at our universities. They've excelled in our sports arenas. They've won Nobel Prizes, built our tallest building and lit the Olympic torch. And when the first Muslim American was recently elected to Congress, he took the oath to defend our Constitution using the same holy Koran that one of our founding fathers, Thomas Jefferson, kept in his personal library."

Obama's interpretation of America's history was, as usual, bizarre.

> "Sorry, Barack Hussein, but there were no Muslims among the passengers on the Mayflower or the settlers at Jamestown. Muslims were conspicuously absent from the ranks of George Washington's Army of the Revolution and played no role in the creation of the American republic save for the fact that the new country's first declaration of war was against the forces of Islam in the form of the Barbary pirates. (5)

Obama's Cairo speech was rife with factual inaccuracies. Just as he did with his own personal narrative, Obama is entirely comfortable either rewriting history or with his own abysmal ignorance of it as long as it advances his personal agenda.

> "We live in an era on which those who actually know and
> study history are becoming a vanishing breed. Instead, we
> embrace "narratives" that play fast and loose with even the
> most ascertainable facts in order to maintain a favored reading
> of political and historical events, in other words, to reinforce
> our prejudices or emotional needs. We do not scruple to
> invent "truths" if necessary and, as if we were reprising the
> antics of Procrustes, have no compunction in either racking or
> dismembering the annals of the past. In the contemporary
> milieu, it is almost as if having truth on one's side—
> demonstrable truth—is a liability or a very weak ally, a
> highwayman's quarry." (6)

David Solway perfectly illustrates the disastrous effects of a combination of intractable ignorance dispensed by our public schools combined with intentional revisionism to support comfortable misperceptions without regard to their truths.

This is much the same way activist judges operate. The activist jurist determines the desired outcome and then sets about manipulating facts and bending the law to the extent necessary to justify the ruling. The ethical and competent judge determines the facts impartially and applies the law to the set of facts without an effort to fashion a particular outcome consistent with his own ideology.

The Left has created mythologies about America and social justice which are in direct contradiction to historical facts. Rather than acknowledge the truth, the liberal resorts to distorting and misrepresenting the facts to support his false narrative.

> "As a result, the crisis in which the West now finds itself is
> largely one of its own making and is rooted primarily in the false
> relation it has entered into with history. Its response to the
> tangled exigencies of the contemporary world is grounded in a

willful and Procrustean tendency to reconfigure the past in such a way as to decomplexify or distort the issues which confront and environ us. In effect, we lay the past upon the iron bed of our received assumptions and then proceed to adjust it to the frame's dimensions. The past is consequently made to conform to the mold of the West's majority prejudices while at the same time appearing to offer an explanation for the convolutions of the present—which for this reason remain unamenable to our best efforts at understanding and amelioration." (7)

Radical revisionism accelerated in the 1960's protest era. The decaying hippies of that era are responsible both for dumbing down your kids and preaching entirely false historical doctrine in which the United States is cast as the center of all that is evil and unjust in the world.

"Times change as do official government policies, yet America gets no credit for ending the despotic regime of a mass murderer like Saddam Hussein, for attacking the Taliban in Afghanistan and scrubbing out the al-Qaeda bases and training camps which threatened an entire world, or for coming to the defense of Muslim populations in Kuwait, Bosnia, and Kosovo. That the United States is the largest contributor to the budget of the United Nations and shouldered the lion's share of the relief efforts in tsunami-stricken Southeast Asia does not absolve it from universal disdain. In restricting America to one or another given period in its evolution as a nation and so assigning it a fixed narrative identity, the *soi-disant* "enlightened" free world cannot accept that America under Reagan, and to some extent under Bush *père et fils*, had opened a new era in global strategy, making its interests approximately identical with its values." (8)

Thus whether Obama is simply appallingly ignorant of American history or just another radical revisionist, America was quite willing to go along with his distorted, blame America first ideology.

Evidently, Obama was also absent the day the history of the Cold War was taught. On a recent visit to Russia, Obama once again claimed moral equivalency between the United States and yet another brutal regime, the former Soviet Union.

The Un-American president consistently fails to speak out against anti-American lies.

> "Speaking to a group of students, our president explained it this way: 'The American and Soviet armies were still massed in Europe, trained and ready to fight. The ideological trenches of the last century were roughly in place. Competition in everything from astrophysics to athletics was treated as a zero-sum game. If one person won, then the other person had to lose. And then within a few short years, the world as it was ceased to be. Make no mistake: This change did not come from any one nation. The Cold War reached a conclusion because of the actions of many nations over many years, and because the people of Russia and Eastern Europe stood up and decided that its end would be peaceful.'" (9)

Actually the Cold War was won because President Ronald Reagan stood absolutely resolute against brutal oppression and tyranny. Reagan took down a thoroughly evil empire that had slaughtered millions of its own citizens while forcing the rest to live in abject misery.

> "The truth, of course, is that the Soviets ran a brutal, authoritarian regime. The KGB killed their opponents or dragged them off to the Gulag. There was no free press, no freedom of speech, no freedom of worship, no freedom of any kind. The basis of the Cold War was not 'competition in astrophysics and athletics.' It was a global battle between tyranny and freedom. The Soviet "sphere of influence" was delineated by walls and barbed wire and tanks and secret police to prevent people from escaping. America was an unmatched force for good in the world during the Cold War. The Soviets were not. The Cold War ended not because the

Soviets decided it should but because they were no match for the forces of freedom and the commitment of free nations to defend liberty and defeat Communism." (10)

Obama's relentless refusal to acknowledge the truth about American history is more than merely offensive, it is dangerous.

"It is irresponsible for an American president to go to Moscow and tell a room full of young Russians less than the truth about how the Cold War ended. One wonders whether this was just an attempt to push 'reset' or maybe to curry favor. Perhaps, most concerning of all, Mr. Obama believes what he said." (11)

Of course, if Obama acknowledged the truth about America and her achievements he would have rendered himself superfluous. Recall from Hoffer's work that a population vulnerable to take over is one that is discontent. If things are not really so bad, it's the cult leader's job to convince you that they are far worse than you could ever know.

Foundations for Failure

"As John O'Sullivan says, any foundation that is not explicitly right-wing will become a radical left-wing organization within a few years. It could be the Association of University Women, the American Association of Retired People, the American Rose Growers, the Foundation for the Study of Railroad Engineers or the Choral Society of Newport Beach. Left-wing radicals swarm to free foundation money, where they can give gigantic grants to one another and they will never have to do a day's work."

Ann Coulter, Author

Operating to destroy America from within is expensive business and at the core of the operation we find the ubiquitous "philanthropic" foundation. The notion of the charitable foundation is that it should operate in the public interest, providing funds for vital programs to make the world a better place.

In reality, the major foundations provide financing and money laundering services for the most virulently radical, anti American and dangerous actors in the world. Edsel Ford started the Ford Foundation in 1936. Henry Ford II resigned from the Board of Trustees in 1977 expressing his profound disgust with the left-wing direction the foundation had taken.

Ford's current agenda is virtually indistinguishable from George Soros's Open Society Institute (OSI) in seeking to erode homeland security, support terrorism and destroy America as we know it to be replaced with a third rate state in a global New World Order.

Bill Ayers's father, Thomas Ayers, was CEO and chairman of Commonwealth Edison as well as a member of numerous other boards. Most disconcertingly, Tom Ayers was on the board at defense giant General Dynamics. He was a man of great personal wealth and connections in the cesspool of Chicago politics. There is no question that the Ayers family foundation connections have been at the core of Obama's ascendancy.

It would take an especially gifted forensic accountant to sort out all of the various interconnections among the major foundations and their smaller satellites such as Annenberg or the Woods Fund. Ann Dunham worked for the Ford Foundation in Indonesia along with the father of Treasury Secretary and tax cheat, Timothy Geithner. Even a cursory analysis of the relationship to the major charitable foundations to the career of Obama proves it is indeed a very small world after all.

The Chicago based Gamaliel Foundation is yet another Obama favorite. Preferring to operate below the radar, Gamaliel is an influential organization in the world of America haters. Stanley Kurtz unearthed the Obama/Gamaliel connection and found it helped to reconcile the image of the smooth Obama with the flamboyant haters in his close inner circle.

> "The Gamaliel connection appears to supply a solution to the
> riddle of Obama's mysterious political persona. On one hand, he
> likes to highlight his days as a community organizer — a
> profession with proudly radical roots in the teachings of

Chicago's Saul Alinsky, author of the highly influential text *Rules for Radicals*. Obama even goes so far as to make the community-organizer image a metaphor for his distinctive conception of elective office. On the other hand, Obama presents himself as a post-ideological, consensus-minded politician who favors pragmatic, common-sense solutions to the issues of the day. How can Obama be radical and post-radical at the same time? Perhaps by deploying Gamaliel techniques. Gamaliel organizers have discovered a way to fuse their Left-extremist political beliefs with a smooth, non-ideological surface of down-to-earth pragmatism: the substance of Jeremiah Wright with the appearance of Norman Vincent Peale. Could this be Obama's secret?" (12)

In essence, Gamaliel operates as a stealthy version of other radical organizations like ACORN, which by design maintains a high visibility.

"The same separatist, anti-American theology of liberation that was so boldly and bitterly proclaimed by Obama's pastor is shared, if more quietly, by Obama's Gamaliel colleagues. The operative word here is 'quietly.' Gamaliel specializes in ideological stealth, and Obama, a master student of Gamaliel strategy, shows disturbing signs of being a sub rosa radical himself. Obama's legislative tactics, as well as his persistent professions of non-ideological pragmatism, appear to be inspired by his radical mentors' most sophisticated tactics. Not only has Obama studied, taught, and apparently absorbed stealth techniques from radical groups like Gamaliel and ACORN, but in his position as a board member of Chicago's supposedly nonpartisan Woods Fund, he quietly funneled money to his radical allies—at the very moment he most needed their support to boost his political career. It's high time for these shadowy, perhaps improper, ties to receive a dose of sunlight." (13)

The underlying ideology of Gamaliel is not really distinguishable from the rest of the radical nutroots movements. America is evil, racist, jingoistic and just plain mean. The Gamaliel folks have little use for traditional charities feeling that they fail to go far enough in forcing the "haves" to part with their income for the benefit of the "have nots."

None of the left wing radical groups ever present really solid solutions for solving social problems. The grand pooh bah of them all, Saul Alinsky never really addressed what was supposed to happen after a successful revolution.

Radicals don't become radical because they have laudable goals to help their fellow man. They become radicals because they have various forms of mental disorders that lend themselves to acting out. In other words, for the majority of radical extremists, the means justify the ends.

Are We in America Yet?

Barack Obama's early academic years in Indonesia and Hawaii were not fertile grounds for the study of American history. Certainly college provided a nearly endless source for misinformation about the country.

Details are scant about Obama's time at Occidental College in California and Columbia University. We know that at Columbia, Obama studied under rabid anti-American, pro-terrorist Edward Said who was eventually discredited for making up his own fictional life story narrative that formed the foundation of his grievances against Israel. (14)

Not surprisingly, Said was close friends with Bill Ayers and Bernadine Dohrn and wrote a glowing dust jacket blurb for Ayers' book, *Fugitive Days*. After Said's death, Ayers continues to speak of him with high praise.

Again, there is virtually nothing in Obama's history to suggest he that he knows very much about the country he is supposed to lead. What we do know is that his closest friends and mentors have almost unanimously been radicals who despise America and see this great nation not as the greatest source of freedom and liberty in the world, but as its most menacing scourge.

Chapter 15

The Obamanutz Cult

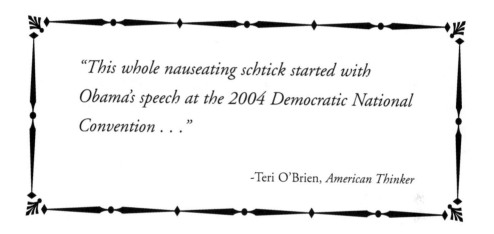

> *"This whole nauseating schtick started with Obama's speech at the 2004 Democratic National Convention . . ."*
>
> -Teri O'Brien, *American Thinker*

Obama beats out Jesus!

A Harris poll in February 2009 reported that Barack Obama had vanquished Jesus Christ as America's number one hero. A sample of 2,634 people was asked whom they admired enough to call their heroes. Obama captured the number one slot which has generally been reserved for Christ the Savior. (1)

During the campaign, a *Chicago Tribune* reporter embarrassed herself and the rest of the nation following Obama around as she prepared to write a book about him entitled *The Savior*. Six people have fainted at Obamafests.

When even the *Rolling Stone* realizes the Obama worship is over-the-top, take heed. While the magazine asserts that there is really no such thing as "Obamaism," we are cautioned not to fall in love with politicians because we will eventually have to give them up. The unabashedly left wing music magazine claims that Obama is not the head of an actual movement, but provides "structure, identity and bases of support." (2)

Surprisingly, the magazine also accedes that Obama has no understanding of foreign policy and has to rely on the "clout of celebrity" and goes on to admit that Obama learned to tell the "story" that would appeal to white women. (3)

Cults have been traditionally studied in the context of religious movements. Thus, some of the more apologetic cult experts have refused to label the Obama Movement as a true cult, but they readily concede that the situation is "cult-like." Lenore Skenazy refers to Obama as the Magic Man; as people feel unable to take control over their own lives, they look to the Magic Man to do it for them. His ambiguity then is intentional allowing his fans to project their own visions and idiosyncrasies; people see what they want to see in Obama. The adoration of Obama was not an intellectual operation; it was built on a shared emotional experience. (4) *New York* magazine defined Obamaism as a "kind of religion," rooted in a deep faith in "rationality." (5)

The feel-good message of hope and change that never becomes too specific provides the perfect Petri dish for cult cultivation; though there are those who believe that Obama never intended to rise to the status of cult leader. (6)

Our inclination to follow charismatic leaders goes back to primitive times when people believed in magic. We really should be past that by now. But the Obamanutz have exalted Obama to the extent that he is not only perceived as the Messiah, but he is exempt from the rules that apply to the rest of us by virtue of his greatness. (7)

In the past, our American leaders' charisma evolved out of their perceived strength. Men like Teddy Roosevelt and Ronald Reagan are admired for their intestinal fortitude. Obama could never pull that one off. He is admired as a healer, not a commander. His popularity is consistent with the Oprafication of America and is well suited for the TV talk show culture. (8)

Sociologist Max Weber describes charisma as a "certain quality in an individual personality by virtue of which he is set apart from ordinary men and treated as endowed with supernatural, superhuman, or at least specifically exceptional powers or qualities." The result is a political swindle, that is, the belief that a charismatic politician can somehow ordain a "civic happy hour," or give people a sense of community that will make them feel less bad. (9)

The Obamanutz cult could never have advanced without the sweeping support of the ministry of propaganda once known as the mainstream media. The rookie senator from Illinois had a few other advantages, not the least of which was a well-financed campaign. His rival, Senator John McCain (R-AZ), was at an enormous financial disadvantage due to Obama's perfidy: candidate Obama reneged on his commitment to accept public financing. The far more honorable McCain lived up to his promise and hobbled himself. The McCain campaign was poorly managed, but that alone was not enough to sweep Obama into the White House with the fanfare generally reserved for coronations.

Former CBS newsman, Bernard Goldberg, studied the media's coverage of Obama and describes it as a "slobbering love affair." It's not exactly a revelation that the media leans Left, but the 2008 election went far beyond anything the United States had ever seen. The mainstream media in America has stopped being objective journalists and are now dedicated to effecting social change. "Never in my memory were so many journalists so intent on effecting change as they were during the campaign of 2008," says Goldberg. (10)

The Project for Excellence in Journalism reviewed over 2,400 stories from forty-eight news outlets during a critical six-week period during the campaign: after the national conventions through the final presidential debates in mid October. They found that twenty-nine percent of quotations, assertions and innuendo about Obama were negative; compared to fifty-seven percent of the references to McCain. (11)

MSNBC's Joe Scarborough summed it up: "I'll tell you my biggest fear for Barack Obama. He has been sainted. He is Saint Barack. The same mainstream media that tried so desperately to get him elected has engaged in hyperbole, engaged in exaggeration. They have deified this man while destroying everybody else that got in his path." (12)

Mark Manford of the *San Francisco Chronicle* gushes: "Many spiritually advanced people I know... identify Obama as a Light worker, that rare kind of attuned being who has the ability not merely to lead us... but who can actually help us usher in a new way of being on the planet, of relating and connecting and engaging with this bizarre earthly experiment. These kinds of people actually help us evolve." (13)

Indeed, Obama himself has a limited tolerance for criticism. During the campaign, he kicked three newspaper reporters off his plane and replaced them with reporters from glossy magazines. All three exiled papers—the *Washington Times*, *New York Post*, and *Dallas Morning News*—had endorsed John McCain for president.

The dangers inherent in creating a cult around a politician should be self-explanatory. "It is one thing to be inspired by a social leader whose rhetoric is a call to action and to reorganize. But inspirational power is dangerous when exercised in the political realm." (14) Elevating a politician to Messiah status leads to the risk that the public will fail to hold him accountable. How can Obama be called to account for his numerous missteps when surrounded by an "aura of fanaticism?" (15)

The Obamanutz movement, aided by the ministry of propaganda, propelled a completely unqualified candidate into the White House. Obama certainly was not elected on anything we could describe as merit. His extreme radical ideology and razor-thin resume made him an implausible choice for leader of the free world. America not only elected the Alinsky alum, they created a mass movement around him.

A parent in the Las Vegas area complained that her son was required to say the Pledge of Allegiance to a large picture of Obama alongside the flag. (16) A local sheriff's department in New York State arrested drug dealers for selling "Obama heroin." (17) Obama projects are being assigned by school teachers throughout the land. Obama paraphernalia is everywhere. Your local bookstore likely has an Obama shrine with at least one table covered in Obama books, videos, and assorted trinkets. Only the Chia Obama may not be available in time for the holidays.

Obamabilia may be the only economic stimulus this president actually provides. Presidential historian Barry H. Landau has "never, ever, ever, ever seen this." Landau tracks presidential memorabilia and estimates that Obama has more than four times as many products devoted to him as any past president. While presidential souvenirs date back to George Washington, Landau says Obama gear is in different league in terms of tastelessness. A few examples: "iKiss Barack" lip gloss and Obama condoms bearing the label "No experience necessary." (18)

A Google search for Barack Obama yields 107 million hits.

Once in office, Obama wasted no time in using his democrat majority congress to push his manifestly radical agenda, beginning with the largest transfer of wealth from the private sector to the government in the history of the nation, lovingly referred to as porkulus. The opposition was effectively shut out of the process. These are the actions of a tyrant.

And when the peasants started to get a little annoying, asking questions about the messiah's pork project, Obama hit the road and did what he does best. Actually it's the only thing he knows how to do: he went back into campaign mode. He did a spectacular job of identifying for us exactly the kind of people who are most vulnerable to a cult leader. Young Julio of Fort Myers, doing his "I'm not worthy!" shtick, provides us a glimpse into the psyche of a true believer.

Cynical types could make comparisons to the ubiquitous portraits of various and sundry dictators found in countries with less than free populations.

Breaking Up Is Hard to Do: Help, I Still Love My Abuser!

Ending a love affair with a narcissist is even harder than ending a healthy relationship. Narcissists don't take it well. As Bernard Goldberg put it, many Americans are "dumb and in love" with Barack Obama. The true believers continue to pose as members of an objective media, all the while being led around by the nose by the *New York Times*.

But despite the best efforts of the mainstream media to keep the Obamanutz cult alive, at least a few Americans are starting to question both Obama's competency and motives. While it is in our nature to look for the happy ending and believe that the good guys will ultimately prevail, dismantling a cult is a large-scale project. There will be no Perry Mason moment in which the truth is revealed about Obama, and the nation comes to its senses. Directly challenging the true believer makes him dig his heels in deeper. The one truth about cults or mass movements is that the outcome depends on the character of the leader. They often end badly.

Conservative commentator Rush Limbaugh told Sean Hannity that we have lost the pop culture. He's right. The coarsening of our culture and moral decline both work in Obama's favor. Bernard Goldberg reminds us of the power wielded by the mainstream media, which remains entirely devoted to Obama, a man who is angry at our Founding Fathers over slavery and our allies over colonialism and holds numerous grudges against the United States. Limbaugh admonishes that there will be no happy endings until pop culture is reformed.

Reaching out to young people is imperative. Not all college students are comfortable with the replacement of academics with indoctrination. Many kids are bright enough to know they are being manipulated. They need a place to go for support. Conservative groups can be found even on the most extremely radical college campuses. Young people want to fit in and feel a sense of belonging; we need to engage with them, lest they fall victim to the same radicalization afflicting their less intelligent counterparts.

Billionaire Warren Buffet and others in the financial community are sounding like battered wives. They express their trepidation over Obama's economic policies while yammering about how they still "love the guy." According to Goldberg, they really do. Half of America is dumb and in love.

Demystifying the cult leader's power is crucial to recovery. This task is made especially trying by the relentlessness of the mainstream media in its efforts to protect the messiah. As Rush Limbaugh has observed, Obama, like some of our major financial institutions, is simply too big to fail. The media won't allow it.

Abusive relationships are more difficult to end than healthy ones. Our relationship to a president who lies to us and betrays the sovereignty of the nation is, unquestionably, abusive. Bonds formed through traumatic events are far more durable than bonds forged via healthy interactions. (19) The toady press has a great deal invested in Obama. It is not farsighted to expect they will abandon their mission anytime soon.

Obama and his left wing congress are making it no secret that they want to shut down the alternative media, especially talk radio, one of the only outlets for opinions that diverge from Dear Leader's. The Obama White House has used its power and prestige to harass private citizens who disagree with Obama.

Expect the illusions about Obama's powers and good intentions to persist in defiance of objective reality. Obama could be found standing over a dead body with a smoking gun, and nothing would come of it. Half of America is dumb and in love.

There are persistent demands for proof of Obama's constitutional eligibility to be President of the United States. The Birthers, as they are called, have launched numerous challenges to Obama's citizenship. To date, Obama has spent nearly a million dollars defending various lawsuits rather than address the issue directly and release his birth certificate and the passport he used to travel to Pakistan in the 1980s.

Americans are startled to discover just how minimal the requirements are for attaining the highest office in the land. Our Founding Fathers left it up to the citizens to vet their candidates. We should be able to rely on a media antagonistic to all politician as well as the parties themselves to do a thorough examination of those who aspire to high office.

The plenary degradation of the mainstream press has put the United States in the unimaginable circumstance of having a president who could not qualify for a basic security clearance. The President of the United States is not required to have a security clearance.

Barry Doesn't Need No Stinkin' Security Clearance!

How perplexing it is that the leader of the free world and possessor of the nuke codes is not required to have a national security clearance. An Army private who may come into contact with classified documents must be cleared. The Commander in Chief is exempt from any such scrutiny.

The president also decides who within his administration should be cleared and at what level.

In 1995, Bill Clinton issued Executive Order 12958-Classified National Security Information, as Amended. To no one's astonishment, Clinton amended the previous order to facilitate the declassification of information. With emblematic liberal disregard for threats to the nation's security, Clinton's order required that classifiers would have to "justify" the classification of any information. Employees would be "encouraged" to challenge "improper" classification.

In a press release dated April 17, 1995, Clinton said: "We will no longer tolerate the excesses of the current system. For example, we will resolve doubtful calls about classification in favor of keeping the information unclassified."

Setting aside for the moment, the hilarity of Clinton condemning excesses, the message was fairly unambiguous. Radical left wing groups cheered Clinton's move as an unmistakable cue that the country's security was likely to be compromised.

In 2003, President Bush amended 12958 by Executive Order 13292. The bulk of Clinton's order remained intact. Bush did, however, remove the burden on government employees who sought classification of foreign information. Bush also expanded the authority of the vice president in making decisions about classification of sensitive information. Plainly, Bush, like the rest of us, never foresaw a Vice President Joe Biden.

Nor did anyone presage that the American people would install a national security risk in the White House. Lamentably, the President of the United States has the authority to classify information or delegate classification authority.

Thus, Obama is free to appoint any unhinged radical he chooses to a position which will provide access to sensitive security data. Rosa Brooks is a sterling example of the species with which Obama will infest our government. Soros lackey and former *Los Angeles Times* columnist, Brooks is Obama's choice for adviser to Under Secretary of Defense for Policy, Michelle Fluronoy. Brooks describes the appointment as her own personal government bailout. How reassuring that Fluronoy holds one of the most powerful posts in the Pentagon.

Brooks was Special Counsel for Soros's Open Society Institute and was an adviser to the virulently transnational Harold Koh. Chronically incensed at America, Brooks used her column to issue invectives against the United States and the Bush Administration. Liberals are not celebrated for their originality of thought.

It's happened to us before. After World War II, we dropped our guard and ended up with Soviet spies worming their way into the highest levels of government.

In 1995 the CIA released decoded Soviet communiqués known as the Verona cables which turned out to be most revealing. After decades of liberals savaging the reputation of Senator Joseph McCarthy, almost no one other than authors Ann Coulter and M. Stanton Evans are talking about the Verona discoveries which vindicate McCarthy. Liberals to this day don't understand that McCarthy's sole mission was to uncover Soviet operatives working in government positions, not put insipid movie actors out of work. In fact, being blacklisted in Hollywood became a badge of honor. For all of their bleating about "McCarthyism", the left never has understood that McCarthy was a senator and their jeremiad should be directed toward the House Un-American Activities Committee (HUAC).

Soviet spies were allowed to run wild, handing over sensitive information, including nuclear secrets, to the Kremlin. We dodged a nuclear bullet thanks to the resoluteness of Ronald Reagan.

Do not expect continued economic trouble to be Obama's undoing. To do so would ignore history: FDR kept getting reelected despite the fact that unemployment never dropped below ten percent on his watch. At times, the jobless rate was as high as seventeen-to-nineteen percent. Obama has co-opted FDR's inclination to blame his predecessor for all of his problems. As long as FDR made people feel good, the public supported him.

There is some cause for optimism with the recent release of polling data showing a gap between Obama's personal popularity and support for his policies. Evidently, Americans understand that his policies are dreadful, but like the guy anyway. Joseph Stalin's current sixty percent approval rating suggests a similar pattern. Presumably, those who still like Stalin personally disapprove of his slaughter of millions of innocent citizens.

We won't get out of this mess by doing what we've been doing. The loyal opposition has ceased to be either. The Republican Party is no longer distinguishable from the Democrat Party. The Republicans have strayed too far from their roots. The current crop of Republicans in Congress has forgotten about the United States Constitution. Rush Limbaugh gets it exactly right: The Republicans have abandoned principles in favor of policies. It's easy to get lost that way. Our founding principles are beautifully enunciated in the United States Constitution. Those who should know better have allowed the *New York Times* and the rest of the left wing cabal to convince them that the way to win hearts and minds is to abandon conservative principles and be "moderates." The Republicans seem hell-bent on sticking with this moderate business, despite two disastrous elections. Nobody honors the great moderates in history.

Lackadaisical America has allowed too much power to be concentrated in Washington DC, which is the entirely contradictory to what our Founding Fathers had in mind. The Constitution sets manifest limits on the power that can be taken by the central government; all rights not *expressly* granted to the federal government belong to the individual states. Activist judges have overreached for decades, incrementally expanding the power of the politicians in DC to create what functions more like a politburo than the comparatively weak central authority envisioned by our founders. They understood the dangers inherent in concentrating power in one central body. It took a long and bloody revolution to escape that kind of tyranny.

Washington DC politicians cannot fix Washington DC. To survive Obama's reign requires that the citizenry reduce, to the extent possible, dependency on the federal government. Some states have already passed resolutions affirming their sovereignty. The more the individual citizen becomes active in exerting influence over their state and local governments, the easier it will become to take our constitutionally granted power back.

Those unfamiliar with the US Constitution get suckered into believing that the federal government needs our money to fund "vital" programs. The vital programs that the federal government is supposed to be funding are the military, controlling the borders and interstate commerce. You will note that the Obama administration wants no part of the first two.

Our founders understood that giving the government too much power would lead inevitably to tyranny. That is why the Constitution grants very limited powers to the central government, and all other powers belong to the individual states.

This is where conservatives are so often and wrongly accused of being heartless. It is not that the strict constructionalist, that is, one who believes the Constitution is to be interpreted as it is written, lacks compassion. Nobody is arguing against programs to help Americans in need. What is unconstitutional is the confiscation of private property by way of oppressive taxation by a central government.

If you live in Hastings, Nebraska, why should you be forced to pay for a new dog park in San Francisco? Or a new monument in Gary, Indiana? If the good people of those communities need a new park, the onus should be on them to find a way to fund it. There are plenty of options; the people can debate it at the city or county level; perhaps they will decide to put it on the local ballot and raise property taxes or issue bonds to pay for these local projects. Only the people in the communities know what is best for their own communities not some politician in Washington DC.

Given the opportunity, private citizens, charities, and businesses *always* get the job done more efficiently and with lower costs than a bloated, bureaucrat-driven, central government. When the government gets out of the way, private industry becomes innovative in solving not only business problems, but in contributing to the community. Limbaugh, in his CPAC 2009 speech, elucidates it perfectly: true conservatives are the most compassionate people in the world. A conservative wants everyone to succeed, to prosper, and to realize their dreams. What our politicians should be doing is removing roadblocks to those dreams and getting out of the way. An oppressive, bloated central government can never facilitate individual freedom.

There are not many limits to what local citizens should be able to do within their own communities. The benefit of keeping as much of your government close to home is that if your representatives mismanage, you citizens can show up at city council meetings and express your displeasure. You, as a citizen have a lot more power over your town council than you do over your "representatives" in DC. Mounting a campaign against a corrupt or ineffectual local representative is easier and far less expensive than trying to clear the deadwood out of Washington.

Our Founding Fathers completely understood this. Each state would have its own specific needs, based on a number of variables, including its unique geography, and the citizens were the best equipped to deal with them.

Washington is now infested not with citizen legislators but with career politicians who are controlled by special interests and their own self-interest. They are far removed from the people who pay their salaries. They have become openly contemptuous of the citizenry, and many no longer even pretend to have an interest in input from those who elected them. This is why DC politicians, with only a few exceptions, have become so arrogant and reckless. They really do believe they are better than you are; they know better than you do and are not far removed from the ruling elite found in every totalitarian state. It won't be easy, but America is well past due for term limits on members of the House and Senate.

While we can be assured that Obama's policies will be disastrous for the nation, relying on the current administration to screw things up is not a winning platform for the opposition party. The loyal opposition must return to core principles and present a clearly defined alternative. We should anticipate ever increasing attempts to squelch opposing voices as at least some Americans begin to see Obama for who and what he is.

Parents must become fully engaged in their children's education. If your kids are in Ayers-based public schools, it is essential that you review each of your child's textbooks. Be on guard for distortions regarding the history of Christianity and its often-unfavorable treatment when compared to Islam. Inject yourself into your child's education. Parents can exert power over their local school board. Parental apathy aided and abetted Obama's taking of the White House.

It is heartening to see so many influential conservatives Rush Limbaugh, Sean Hannity, Glenn Beck, Mark Levin, and others getting the word out about tea party protests sprouting up all over the country. Those are exactly the type of grassroots movements that send the unambiguous message that Americans are still willing to stand up for individual liberty and will resist the tyranny that the current administration is hell-bent on forcing on us.

At the time of writing this book, conservatives are casting about for new leadership, and many have become dispirited by the failure of a shiny new leader to appear. Conservative radio talk show host, Tammy Bruce, sagely observed that conservatives are by nature difficult to lead. Conservatism celebrates and honors individualism and personal responsibility. Conservatism does not lend itself to being taken over by a charismatic cult figure.

The elections in 2010 are likely our last chance to slow down the destruction of democracy as we have known it. If we foolishly reelect the same politicians who have allowed the federal government to turn into the behemoth it is today, we will have squandered our liberties for a long time to come, possibly forever. Obama's policies with regard to bloodthirsty terrorists devoted to our destruction makes it imperative that we replace the current inept politicians with focused, principled, and patriotic Americans with the courage to challenge the narcissist in chief and his cronies.

As is typical for codependents in unhealthy relationships, many Obamanutz are beginning to understand how bad he is for America, but cling to the idea that it will get better. He won't. Tyrants and messiahs never take responsibility for the damage they do. "When a messianic leader is faced with failure, his tendency is to castigate the people, or his political opposition, or the media as evil and to continue on unmoved and bring his country down with him." (20)

As the casualties mount up, do not expect Obama to have an epiphany and turn the country back into the United States as our Founding Fathers meant it to be.

Soviet defector Yuri Bezmenov offers his wisdom about getting America back:

> "Well, the immediate thing that comes to mind is, of course, there must be a very strong national effort to educate people in the spirit of REAL patriotism, number one. Number two, to explain [to] them the real danger of socialist, communist, welfare state, Big Brother government. If people fail to grasp the impending danger; nothing ever will help the United States. You may kiss goodbye your freedoms, including [sending] homosexuals to prison inmate. All this freedom will vanish in 5 seconds - including your precious lives.
>
> The moment at least part of [the] United States population is convinced that the danger is real, they have to FORCE their government, and I'm not talking about sending letters, signing petitions, and all this beautiful, noble activity, I'm talking about FORCING [the] United States government to stop aiding Communism." (21)

Nor is much help on the way from Washington. We the people have to handle this one ourselves.

Notes

Chapter 1: The Essence of Cultism

1. Lalich, Janja, PhD. *Bounded Choice: True Believers and Charismatic Cults.* London: University of California Press, LTD, 2004.
2. Langone, Michael, ed. *Recovering from Cults.* London: WW Norton & Co., 1993.
3. Zablocki, Benjamin and Robbins, Thomas, Eds. "Pitfalls in the Sociological Study of Cults", *Misunderstanding Cults.* Toronto: University of Toronto Press, 2001.
4. Ibid.
5. Landau, Madeline Tobias and Lalich, Janja. *Captive Hearts, Captive Minds: Freedom and Recovery From Cults and Abusive Relationships.* Alameda: Hunter House, Inc, 1974.
6. Hoffer, Eric. *The True Believer: Thoughts on the Nature of Mass Movements.* New York: Harper and Row, 1951.
7. Lalich, Janja, PhD. *Bounded Choice: True Believers and Charismatic Cults.* London: University of California Press, LTD, 2004, Pg. 6.
8. Ibid, Pg. 17
9. Zernike, Kate. "The Charisma Mandate." *The New York Times,* 17 February 2008. <http://www.nytimes.com/2008/02/17/weekinreview/17zernike.html>.
10. Zablocki, Benjamin and Robbins, Thomas, Eds. "Pitfalls in the Sociological Study of Cults", *Misunderstanding Cults.* Toronto: University of Toronto Press, 2001.
11. Hoffer, Eric. *The True Believer: Thoughts on the Nature of Mass Movements.* New York: Harper and Row, 1951.
12. Ibid, Pg. 54.
13. Ibid, Pg. 131.
14. Ibid, Pg. 91.
15. Ibid.
16. Ibid, Pg. 92.
17. Ibid, Pgs. 156-157.
18. Landau, Madeline Tobias and Lalich, Janja. *Captive Hearts, Captive Minds*
19. Freddoso, David. *The Case Against Barack Obama: The Unlikely Rise and Unexamined Agenda of the Media's Favorite Candidate.* Washington, DC: Regnery, 2008, Pg. 89.

Chapter 2: The Fourth Estate in Ruins

1. Goldberg, Bernard. Interview With Bill O'Reilly. *The O'Reilly Factor*. 9 March 2009.

2. Freddoso, David. *The Case Against Barack Obama: The Unlikely Rise and Unexamined Agenda of the Media's Favorite Candidate*. Washington, DC: Regnery, 2008, Pg. 53.

3. Goldberg, Bernard. *A Slobbering Love Affair: The True (and Pathetic) Story of the Torrid Romance Between Barack Obama and the Mainstream Media*. Washington, DC: Regnery Publishing, Inc, 2009, Pg. 30.

4. Ibid.

5. Wallace-Wells, Ben. "Destiny's Child: No Candidate Since Robert F Kennedy Has Sparked as Much Campaign Trail Heat as Barack Obama. But Can the One-Term Senator Craft a Platform to Match His Charisma?" *Rolling Stone*. 22 February 2007. <http://www.rollingstone.com/politics/story/13390609/campaign_08_the_radical_roots_of_barack_obama/3>

6. Cohen, Richard. "Obama's Farrakhan Test." *The Washington Post*. 15 January 2008: Pg. A13. <http://www.washingtonpost.com/wp-dyn/content/article/2008/01/14/AR2008011402083.html>

7. Farrakhan, Louis. "Transcript From Minister Louis Farrakhan's Remarks at the Million Man March". *CNN/US News*. 17 October 1995.

8. <http://www-cgi.cnn.com/US/9510/megamarch/10-16/transcript/index.html>

9. Freddoso, David. *The Case Against Barack Obama: The Unlikely Rise and Unexamined Agenda of the Media's Favorite Candidate*. Washington, DC: Regnery, 2008, Pg. 158.

10. Ibid, Pg. 153.

11. Schmidt, Jeffrey. "The Real Agenda of Black Liberation Theology." *American Thinker*. 19 March 2008. <http://www.americanthinker.com/2008/03/the_real_agenda_of_black_liber.html>

12. Walden, Andrew. "Obama's Other Controversial Church." *Hawai'i Free Press*. 14 June 2009. http://www.hawaiifreepress.com/main/ArticlesMain/tabid/56/articleType/ArticleView/articleId/815/Obamas-Other-Controversial-Church.aspx

13. Kurtz, Stanley. Interview with Hugh Hewitt. 6 October 2008. <http://hughhewitt.townhall.com/blog/g/43474e3d-252a-4011-9044-2befe2e65e40>

14. McCarthy, Andrew C. "The L.A. Times Suppresses Khalidi Bash Tape." *NRO*. 27 October 2008.

<http://article.nationalreview.com/?q=ZDFkMGE2MmM1M2Q5MmY0ZmE
xMzUxMWRhZGJmMTAyOGY

15. Kurtz, Stanley. Interview with Hugh Hewitt. 6 October 2008. <http://hugh
hewitt.townhall.com/blog/g/43474e3d-252a-4011-9044-2befe2e65e40>

16. Hoffler, Eric. *The True Believer: Thoughts on the Nature of Mass Movements.*
New York: Harper and Row, 1951, Pg. 119.

17. Ibid.

18. Ibid, Pgs. 140-141.

Chapter 3: The Great American Dumb Down

1. Blackwell, Ken. "Dumbing Down America." *Townhall.com.* 22 February 2009.
<http://townhall.com/columnists/KenBlackwell/2009/02/22/dumbing_down_
america?page=2>

2. Chavez, Linda. "Dumbing Down Higher Education." *Townhall.com. 11
January 2008.* <http://townhall.com/columnists/LindaChavez/2008/01/11/
dumbing_down_higher_education>

3. Schlafly, Phyllis. "The NEA Spells Out Its Policies." *Eagleforum.com.* August 2008.
Vol. 42, No. 1. <http://www.eagleforum.org/psr/2008/aug08/psraug08.html>

4. Ibid.

5. Ibid.

6. Schlafly, Phyllis. "'Social Justice: Code Word for Anti-Americanism."
Eagleforum.org. January 2009.
<http://www.eagleforum.org/psr/2009/jan09/psrjan09.html>

7. Ibid.

8. "Bill Ayers." *DiscovertheNetworks.org.*
http://www.discoverthenetworks.org/individualProfile.asp?indid=2169

9. Kurtz, Stanley. Interview with Hugh Hewitt. 6 October 2008. <http://hugh
hewitt.townhall.com/blog/g/43474e3d-252a-4011-9044-2befe2e65e40>

10. Grossman, Ron. "Family Ties Proved Ayers' Point." *Chcagotribune.com.*
18 May 2008. <http://www.chicagotribune.com/news/opinion/
chi-radical-ayers_thinkmay18,0,5953909.story>

11. Ibid.

12. Ibid.

13. Ibid.

14. Ibid.

15. Ibid.

16. Kurtz, Stanley. Interview with Hugh Hewitt. 6 October 2008. <http://hugh hewitt.townhall.com/blog/g/43474e3d-252a-4011-9044-2befe2e65e40>

17. Horowitz, David. Interview with Sean Hannity. *Sean Hannity Show.* 9 March 2009.

18. Schlafly, Phyllis. "'Social Justice: Code Word for Anti-Americanism." *Eagleforum.org.* January 2009. <http://www.eagleforum.org/psr/2009/jan09/psrjan09.html> *Ibid.*

19. Ibid.

20. Ibid.

21. Ibid.

Chapter 4: The Putrefied Pop Culture's Pick

1. Pinsky, Drew and Young, S. Mark. *The Mirror Effect: How Celebrity Narcissism is Seducing America.* New York: Harper Collins, 2009, Pg. 62.

2. Ibid.

3. Ibid, Pg. 7.

4. Ibid, Pg. 12.

5. Ibid, Pg. 173.

6. Ibid, Pg. 74.

7. Tibbetts, Graham. "Michael Jackson 'Converts' to Islam and Changes Name to Mikaeel'". *Telegraph.co.uk.* 21 November 2008. http://www.telegraph.co.uk/news/newstopics/celebritynews/3494296/ Michael-Jackson-converts-to-Islam-and-changes-name-to-Mikaeel.html

8. Jackson, Jermaine. *The Religion of Islam.* 16 January 2006. http://www.islamreligion.com/articles/90/

9. Daragahi, Borzou. "Family, Friends Mourn 'Neda", Iranian Woman Who Died on Video." *Los Angeles Times.* 23 June 2009. http://www.latimes.com/news/ nationworld/world/la-fg-iran-neda23-2009jun23,0,366975,full.story

10. Glick, Caroline B. "Obama the Savior". *Jewish World Review.* 22 April 2008. http://www.jewishworldreview.com/0408/glick042208.php3

11. Engber, Andrea. "10 Helpful Hints for Raising a Boy". *IVillage.* http://parenting.ivillage.com/mom/structure/0,,427g,00.html

Chapter 5: Intractable Ignorance

1. Salter, Anna C, PhD. *Predators: Pedophiles, Rapists, and Other Sex Offenders, Who They Are, How They Operate and How We Can Protect Ourselves and Our Children.* New York: Basic Books, 2003.

2. Ibid, Pg. 196.

3. Ibid.
4. Ibid, Pg. 217.
5. Ibid.

Chapter 6: Barry Soetoro: Profiles in Chaos

1. Churcher, Sharon. "A Drunk and a Bigot-What the US Presidential Hopeful HASN'T Said About His Father." *Mail Online.* 27 January 2007. <http://www.dailymail.co.uk/news/article-431908/A-drunk-bigot—US-Presidental-hopefulHASNT-said-father-.html.>

2. Obama, Barack. *Dreams From My Father.* New York: Random House, 1995, Pg. 4.

3. Scharnberg, Kirsten and Barker, Kim. "The Not-So-Simple Story of Barack Obama's Youth". *Chicago Tribune.com.* 25 March 2007. <http://www.chicagotribune.com/news/nationworld/chi-0703250359 mar25-archive,0,546290.story>

4. Obama, Barack. *The Audacity of Hope: Thoughts on Reclaiming the American Dream.* New York: Crown Publishers, 2006, Pg. 203.

5. Friedman, Herbert A. SGM (Ret.) "Psyop of the Mau-Mau Uprising". *Psywar.org.* 22 February 2009. <http://www.psywar.org/maumau.php>

6. Ibid.

7. Staff. "The Oath Takers". *Time.* 13 June 1960. <http://www.time.com/time/printout/0,8816,940578,00.html>

8. Ripley, Amanda. "The Story of Barack Obama's Mother." *Time.* 9 April 2008. <http://www.time.com/time/nation/article/0,8599,1729524,00.html>

9. Staff, *Wall Street Journal Online.* "Suharto's Indonesia." 28 January 2008. http://online.wsj.com/article/SB120147370239720549.html?mod=opinion_main_europe_asia#articleTabs=article

10. Ikenga, L.E. "Obama, the African Colonial." *American Thinker.* 25 June 2009. http://www.americanthinker.com/2009/06/obama_the_african_colonial.html

11. Obama, Barack. *The Audacity of Hope: Thoughts on Reclaiming the American Dream.* New York: Crown Publishers, 2006.

12. Ibid, Pg. 273. <http://www.telegraph.co.uk/news/worldnews/northamerica/usa/barackobama/2601914/Frank-Marshall-Davis-alleged-Communist-was-early-influence-on-Barack-Obama.html>

Chapter 7: Dreams from My Father, Pathology from My Mother

1. Ikenga, L.E. "Obama, the African Colonial." *American Thinker.* 25 June 2009. http://www.americanthinker.com/2009/06/obama_the_african_colonial.html

2. Ibid.
3. Walden, Andrew. "Barack Obama: Red Diaper Baby." *American Thinker.* 30 October 2008. http://www.americanthinker.com/2008/10/barack_obama_ red_diaper_baby_1.html
4. Ibid.
5. Ibid.
6. *Dreams*, pg. 51.
7. Dewey, Alice and White, Geoffrey. "Ann Dunham: A Personal Reflection." Anthropology *News.* November 2008.
   http://www.anthropology.hawaii.edu/News/Announcements/2008/dunham.html
8. Ibid.
9. Discoverthenetworks.org. "Ford Foundation."
   http://www.discoverthenetworks.org/funderProfile.asp?fndid=5176
10. Dewey and White.

Chapter 8: The Narcissist in Chief

1. "Narcissistic Personality Disorder." *Encyclopedia of Mental Disorders: Ka-Nu.* http://www.minddisorders.com/Kau-Nu/Narcissistic-personality-disorder.html.
2. Pinsky, Drew and Young, S. Mark. *The Mirror Effect: How Celebrity Narcissism is Seducing America.* New York: Harper Collins, 2009.
3. Fabrizio, Lisa. "The MTV President." *The American Spectator.* 25 March 2009. http://spectator.org/archives/2009/03/25/the-mtv-president
4. Ibid.
5. Pinsky, Drew and Young, S. Mark. *The Mirror Effect: How Celebrity Narcissism is Seducing America.* New York: Harper Collins, 2009, Pgs. 98-99.
6. Vaknin, Sam, PhD. "Barak Obama-Narcissist or Merely Narcissistic?" *Global Politician.* 13 August 2008.
   <http://www.globalpolitician.com/25109-barack-obama-elections>.
7. McKenzie, David. "Behind the Scenes: Meet George Obama." *CNN.com.* 22 August 2008. <http://www.cnn.com/2008/POLITICS/08/22/bts.obama.brother/>.
8. Obama, Barack. *The Audacity of Hope: Thoughts on Reclaiming the American Dream.* New York: Crown Publishers, 2006, Pg. 322.
9. Churcher, Sharon. "A Drunk and a Bigot-What the US Presidential Hopeful HASN'T Said About His Father." *Mail Online.* 27 January 2007.
   <http://www.dailymail.co.uk/news/article-431908/A-drunk-bigot—US-Presidental-hopefulHASNT-said-father-.html

10. Vaknin, Sam, PhD. "Barak Obama-Narcissist or Merely Narcissistic?" *Global Politician*. 13 August 2008. <http://www.globalpolitician.com/25109-barack-obama-elections>.

11. Ibid.

12. Sina, Ali. "Understanding Obama: the Making of a Fuehrer." 22 September 2008. FaithFreedom.org. <http://www.faithfreedom.org/obama.html>.

13. Gutman, Stephanie. "Barack Obama's Problem." *Telegraph.co.uk*. 8 March 2009. <http://blogs.telegraph.co.uk/stephanie_gutmann/blog/2009/03/08/barack_obamas_problem>

14. Ibid.

15. Pinsky, Drew and Young, S. Mark. *The Mirror Effect: How Celebrity Narcissism is Seducing America*. New York: Harper Collins, 2009.

16. Ibid.

17. Ibid, Pg. 92.

18. Ibid.

19. Ibid.

20. Ibid.

21. Ibid.

22. Ibid, pg. 93.

23. Ibid, Pg. 95.

24. Ibid.

Chapter 9: Uncle Frankie

1. Harnden, Toby. "Frank Marshall Davis, Alleged Communist Was Early Influence on Barack Obama." *Telegraph.co.uk*. *24 August 2008*. *http://www.telegraph.co.uk/news/worldnews/northamerica/usa/barack obama/2601914/Frank-Marshall-Davis-alleged-Communist-was-early-influence-on-Barack-Obama.html*

2. Walton, Andrew. "The Frank Marshall Davis Network." *Accuracy in Media*. 1 September 2008. <http://www.aim.org/aim-report/the-frank-marshall-davis-network/>.

3. Ibid.

4. Harnden, Toby. "Frank Marshall Davis, Alleged Communist Was Early Influence on Barack Obama." *Telegraph.co.uk*. *24 August 2008*. http://www.telegraph.co.uk/news/worldnews/northamerica/usa/barackobama/2601914/Frank-Marshall-Davis-alleged-Communist-was-early-influence-on-Barack-Obama.html

5. Walden, Andrew. "The Frank Marshall Davis Network." *Accuracy in Media.* 1 September 2008.
    http://www.aim.org/aim-report/the-frank-marshall-davis-network/

6. Harnden, Toby. "Barack Obama's True Colors: The Making of the Man Who Would be US President." *Telegraph.co.uk.* 4 November 2008.
    http://www.telegraph.co.uk/news/worldnews/northamerica/usa/barackobama/2591139/Barack-Obamas-true-colours-The-making-of-the-man-who-would-be-US-president.html

7. Harnden, Toby. "Frank Marshall Davis, Alleged Communist Was Early Influence on Barack Obama." *Telegraph.co.uk.* 24 August 2008.
    http://www.telegraph.co.uk/news/worldnews/northamerica/usa/barack obama/2601914/Frank-Marshall-Davis-alleged-Communist-was-early-influence-on-Barack-Obama.html

8. Kengor, Paul. "Dreams From Frank Marshall Davis." *American Thinker.* 30 October 2008. <http://www.americanthinker.com/2008/10/dreams_from_frank_marshall_dav.html>)

9. Evens, M. Stanton. *Blacklisted By History: The Untold Story of Senator Joe McCarthy and His Fight Against America's Enemies.* New York: Crown Publishing Group, 2007.

10. Ibid, Pg. 20.

11. Ibid, Pg. 21.

12. Obama, Barack. *Dreams From My Father.* New York: Random House, 1995, Pg. 16.

13. Harnden, Toby. "Frank Marshall Davis, Alleged Communist Was Early Influence on Barack Obama." *Telegraph.co.uk.* 24 August 2008.
    http://www.telegraph.co.uk/news/worldnews/northamerica/usa/barack obama/2601914/Frank-Marshall-Davis-alleged-Communist-was-early-influence-on-Barack-Obama.html

Chapter 10: Saul Alinsky: Master Agitator

1. Schlafly, Phyllis. "How a Community Organizer Became President." *Eagleforum.org.* February 2009. Vol. 42, No 7.
    <http://www.eagleforum.org/psr/2009/feb09/psrfeb09.html>

2. Alinsky, Saul D. *Rules for Radicals: A Pragmatic Primer for Realistic Radicals.* Toronto: Random House, 1971. Pg. 127.

3. Ibid.

4. Freddoso, David. *The Case Against Barack Obama: The Unlikely Rise and Unexamined Agenda of the Media's Favorite Candidate.* Washington, DC: Regnery, 2008.

5. Schlafly, Phyllis. "How a Community Organizer Became President." *Eagleforum.org.* February 2009. Vol. 42, No 7.
<http://www.eagleforum.org/psr/2009/feb09/psrfeb09.html> Schlafly,

6. Alinsky, Saul D. *Rules for Radicals: A Pragmatic Primer for Realistic Radicals.* Toronto: Random House, 1971.

7. Ibid, Pgs. 194-195.

8. Schlafly, Phyllis. "How a Community Organizer Became President." *Eagleforum.org.* February 2009. Vol. 42, No 7.
<http://www.eagleforum.org/psr/2009/feb09/psrfeb09.html>

9. Ibid.

10. Ibid.

11. Ibid.

12. Hoffer, Eric. *The True Believer: Thoughts on the Nature of Mass Movements.* New York: Harper and Row, 1951.

13. Alinsky, Saul D. *Rules for Radicals: A Pragmatic Primer for Realistic Radicals.* Toronto: Random House, 1971. Pg. 128.

14. Schlafly, Phyllis. "How a Community Organizer Became President." *Eagleforum.org.* February 2009. Vol. 42, No 7.
http://www.eagleforum.org/psr/2009/feb09/psrfeb09.html

15. Ibid.

16. Freddoso, David. *The Case Against Barack Obama: The Unlikely Rise and Unexamined Agenda of the Media's Favorite Candidate.* Washington, DC: Regnery, 2008.

17. "Cloward-Piven Strategy". *DiscovertheNetworks.org.*
http://www.discoverthenetworks.org/groupProfile.asp?grpid=6967

18. Chandler, Robert. "Chandler" The Cloward-Piven Strategy". *The Washington Times.* 15 October 2008.
http://www.washingtontimes.com/news/2008/oct/15/the-cloward-piven-strategy/

19. "Cloward-Piven Strategy". *DiscovertheNetworks.org.*
http://www.discoverthenetworks.org/groupProfile.asp?grpid=6967

20. Ibid.

21. Ibid.

22. Fund, John. *Stealing Elections.* New York: Encounter Books, 2004, 2008. (Pgs 59-60)

23. Ibid.

24. Ibid, Pg. 48.

25. Ibid, Pg. 61

26. Alinsky, Saul D. *Rules for Radicals: A Pragmatic Primer for Realistic Radicals.* Toronto: Random House, 1971. Pgs. 130-138.

27. Ibid, Pgs. 130-138.

28. Horowitz, David. Interview with Sean Hannity. *Sean Hannity Show.* 9 March 2009.

29. York, Byron. "What Did Obama Do as a Community Organizer?" *National Review Online.* 8 September 2008. http://article.nationalreview.com/print/?q=OWMxNGUxZWJjYzg1NjA0MTl mZDZmMjUwZGU3ZjAwNmU=

Chapter 11: George Soros: International Man of Misery

1. Horowitz, David and Poe, Richard. *The Shadow Party: How George Soros, Hillary Clinton and Sixties Radicals Seized Control of the Democratic Party.* Nashville: Thomas Nelson, Inc., 2006.

2. Ibid.

3. Shriver, Kyle-Anne. "The Religious Quest of George Soros." *The American Thinker.* 10 October, 2007. http://www.americanthinker.com/2007/10/the_religious_quest_of_george.html

4. Soros, George. Interview With Steve Kroft. *60 Minutes.* CBS. 20 December 1998.

5. Mail Foreign Service. *Mail Online.* "'I'm Having a Very Good Crisis,' says Soros as Hedge Fund Managers Make Billions Off Recession." 25 March 2009. http://www.dailymail.co.uk/news/worldnews/article-1164771/Im-having-good-crisis-says-hedge-fund-manager-1billion-world-plunged-recession.html# (176)

6. Horowitz, David and Poe, Richard. *The Shadow Party: How George Soros, Hillary Clinton and Sixties Radicals Seized Control of the Democratic Party.* Nashville: Thomas Nelson, Inc., 2006. (86)

7. Ibid.

8. Ibid.

9. Ibid, Pg. 95

10. Ehrenfeld, Rachel and Macomber, Shawn. "The Man Who Would Be Kingmaker, Part I." *Frontpagemag.com.* 28 October 2004. http://www.frontpagemag.com/articles/Read.aspx?GUID=2BFC76F7-CF8E-4329-8DDA-78579A6F0D21

11. Ibid.

12. Poe, Richard Lawrence. "George Soros' Coup: Soros Vows to 'Puncture' American Supremacy." *Newsmax.* 10 August 2006. http://www.poe.com/2006/08/10/george-soros-coup/

13. Ibid.

14. Horowitz, David and Poe, Richard. *The Shadow Party: How George Soros, Hillary Clinton and Sixties Radicals Seized Control of the Democratic Party.* Nashville: Thomas Nelson, Inc., 2006.

15. Artikkelen, Del denne. "George Soros' Agenda for Drug Legalization, Death, and Welfare." *Fmr.no.* 15 January 1997. http://www.fmr.no/george-soros-agenda-for-drug-legalization-death-and-welfare.78404-10285.html

Chapter 12: Depraved Cult Leaders of Yore

1. Campbell, Susan Bartoletti. *Hitler Youth: Growing Up in Hitler's Shadow.* New York: Scholastic, Inc. 2005, Pg. 19.

2. Nizkor Project. "Hitler as the German People Knew Him." http://www.nizkor.org/hweb/people/h/hitler-adolf/oss-papers/text/oss-profile-02.html.

3. The Nizkor Project. "Hitler as he Believes Himself to Be." http://www.nizkor.org/hweb/people/h/hitler-adolf/oss-papers/text/oss-profile-01.html.

4. Nizkor Project. "Hitler as the German People Knew Him." http://www.nizkor.org/hweb/people/h/hitler-adolf/oss-papers/text/oss-profile-02.html.

5. Lewis, James. "How the Great Depression Brought Adolf Hitler to Power." *American Thinker.* 8 March 2009. http://www.americanthinker.com/2009/03/how_the_great_depression_broug.html

6. Miller, Alice, PhD. "Adolf Hitler: How Could a Monster Succeed in Building a Nation." *The Natural Child Project.* 1998. http://www.naturalchild.com/alice_miller/adolf_hitler.html.

7. Ibid.

8. Goldberg, Jonah. *Liberal Fascism.* New York: Random House, Inc, 2007, Pg. 211.

9. Ibid.

10. Ibid, Pgs 277-278.

11. Ibid, Pg 282.

12. Ibid, Pg. 359.

13. Ibid, Pg. 147.

14. Lewis, James. "How the Great Depression Brought Adolf Hitler to Power." *American Thinker.* 8 March 2009. http://www.americanthinker.com/2009/03/how_the_great_depression_broug. html (149)

15. Campbell, Susan Bartoletti. *Hitler Youth: Growing Up in Hitler's Shadow.* New York: Scholastic, Inc. , Pg. 20.

16. Nizkor Project. "Hitler as the German People Knew Him." http://www.nizkor.org/hweb/people/h/hitler-adolf/oss-papers/text/oss-profile-02.html.

17. Kopel, Dave. "Hitler's Control." *National Review Online.* 22 May 2003. http://www.nationalreview.com/kopel/kopel052203.asp

18. Nizkor Project. "Hitler as the German People Knew Him." http://www.nizkor.org/hweb/people/h/hitler-adolf/oss-papers/text/oss-profile-02.html. (40)

19. Campbell, Susan Bartoletti. *Hitler Youth: Growing Up in Hitler's Shadow.* New York: Scholastic, Inc. 2005, Pgs. 62-63.

20. Heck, Alfons. *A Child of Hitler: Germany in the Days When God Wore a Swastika.* Phoenix: Renaissance House Publishers, 1985, Pg. 202.

21. Ibid.

22. Ibid.

23. Ibid, Pg. 205.

24. Ibid, Pg. 207.

25. Carnes, Patrick J PhD. *The Betrayal Bond: Breaking Free of Exploitive Relationships.* Deerfield Beach, FL: Health Communications, Inc, 1997.

26. Emanuel, Rahm and Reed, Bruce. *The Plan: Big Ideas for America.* New York: Perseus Books Group, 2006, Pg. 62.

27. Picket, Kerry. "2006 *New York Daily News* Podcast with Rahm Emanuel on Compulsory Service Plan, Will Media Ignore Again?" *Newsbusters.org.* 11 November 2008. http://newsbusters.org/blogs/kerry-picket/2008/11/11/ben-smith-interview-rahm-emanuel-compulsory-service-plan-will-media-ig.

28. Staff, AP. "Obama: Boost National Service Programs." *MSNBC.* 5 December 2007. http://www.msnbc.msn.com/id/22117627/

29. Tuicille, JT. "Obama's Involuntary Volunteerism." *East Valley Tribune.* 28 September 2008. http://www.eastvalleytribune.com/story/126921.

30. Heck, Alfons. *A Child of Hitler: Germany in the Days When God Wore a Swastika.* Phoenix: Renaissance House Publishers, 1985, Pg. 121.

31. Satter, David. "Stalin's Legacy." *NRO.* 14 March 2008. http://www.nationalre-view.com/comment/comment-satter031403.asp

32. Kern, Gary. "How 'Uncle Joe' Bugged FDR: the Lessons of History." CIA Historical Document. 14 April 2007. https://www.cia.gov/library/center-for-the-study-of-intelligence/csi-publications/csi-studies/studies/vol47no1/article02.html

33. Ibid.

34. Ibid.

35. Rodriguez, Alex. "Russia Rewriting Josef Stalin's Legacy." *Chicagotribune.com.* 17 December 2008. http://www.chicagotribune.com/news/nationworld/chi-russia-stalin_rodriguezdec17,0,2772612.story

36. Satter, David. "Stalin's Legacy." *NRO.* 14 March 2008. http://www.nationalre-view.com/comment/comment-satter031403.asp

37. Rodriguez, Alex. "Russia Rewriting Josef Stalin's Legacy." *Chicagotribune.com.* 17 December 2008. http://www.chicagotribune.com/news/nationworld/chi-russia-stalin_rodriguezdec17,0,2772612.story

38. Reiterman, Tim and Jacobs, John, *Raven: The Untold Story of the Reverend Jim Jones and his People.* New York: Penguin, 1982.

Chapter 13: What's So Bad About Communism Anyway?

1. Zeleny, Jeff. "The President is on the Line to Follow Up on Socialism." *The New York Times.* 7 March 2009. http://www.nytimes.com/2009/03/08/us/politics/08callback.html

2. PWN/NM Editorial Board. "Editorial: Eye on the Prize." 15 July 2008. *Communist Party USA.* http://www.cpusa.org/article/articleview/975/1/147/.

3. Webb, Sam. "Off and Running: Opportunity of a Lifetime." *PoliticalAffairs.net.* 5 February 2009. http://www.politicalaffairs.net/article/articleview/8085/.

4. Chicago DSA. http://www.chicagodsa.org/ngarchive/ng42.html; http://web.archive.org/web/20010906162143/www.chicagodsa.org/ngarchive/ng45.html

5.

6. Freddoso, David. *The Case Against Barack Obama: The Unlikely Rise and Unexamined Agenda of the Media's Favorite Candidate.* Washington, DC: Regnery, 2008.

7. Ibid.

8. Folks, Jeffrey. "My Socialist Past." *American Thinker*. 15 March 2009. http://www.americanthinker.com/2009/03/my_socialist_past.html

9. Satter, David. "Stalin's Legacy." *NRO*. 14 March 2008. http://www.nationalreview.com/comment/comment-satter031403.asp

10. Beran, Michael Knox. "Obama, Shaman." *City Journal*. Summer 2008; Vol. 18, No. 3. http://www.city-journal.org/2008/18_3_obama.html

11. Engles, Friedrich and Marx, Karl. *The Communist Manifesto*. 25 January 2005 (EBook #61).
    http://www.gutenberg.org/catalog/world/readfile?fk_files=165453&pageno=1
    Hoven, Randall. "Bingo! Call it Communism". *American Thinker*. 3 March 2009. http://www.americanthinker.com/2009/03/bingo_call_it_communism_1.html

12. Ibid.

13. Brooks, Arthur C. *Gross National Happiness*. New York, NY: Basic Books, 2008, pg. 90.

14. Ibid, pg. 91.

15. Ibid, pg. 102.

16. Ibid.

17. Ibid, pg. 167.

18. Ibid.

19. Ibid, pg. 205.

20. Ibid.

21. Millegan, Robert. "Audit: Open Your Eyes KGB Officer Explains Russian/NOW Agenda for 'Amerika'." *CIA-drugs*. 5 June 2009. http://www.mail-archive.com/cia-drugs@yahoogroups.com/msg12782.html

22. Ibid.

23. Ibid.

Chapter 14: An Un-American President

1. Tooley, Mark. "Apologizing for Iran." *The American Spectator*. 9 March 2007. http://spectator.org/archives/2007/03/09/apologizing-for-iran

2. Poe, Richard. "The Idiot's Guide to Chinagate." *Newsmax.com*. 27 May 2003. http://archive.newsmax.com/archives/articles/2003/5/26/214938.shtml

3. Walden, Andrew. "The Frank Marshall Davis Network in Hawaii." *Accuracy in Media*. 29 July 2008. http://www.aim.org/aim-column/the-frank-marshall-davis-network-in-hawaii/

4. Obama, Barack. Roundtable Interview of the President by Regional Reporters. 5 June 2009. http://www.whitehouse.gov/the_press_office/Roundtable-Interview-of-the-President-by-Regional-Reporters-Cairo-Egypt-6-4-09/

5. Williams, Paul, PhD. "Obama Bombs History 101." *The Last Crusade.* http://thelastcrusade.org/2009/06/04/obama-bombs-american-history-101/

6. Solway, David. "Procrustean History: Obama Manipulates the Past to Fit the Narrative." *Pajamasmedia.com.* 30 June 2009. http://pajamasmedia.com/blog/procrustean-history-manipulating-the-past-to-fit-the-narrative/

7. Ibid.

8. Ibid.

9. Cheney, Liz. "Obama Rewrites the Cold War." *The Wall Street Journal.* 13 July 2009. http://online.wsj.com/article/SB124744075427029805.html

10. Ibid.

11. Ibid.

12. Kurtz, Stanley. "Senator Stealth." *NRO.* 1 November 2008. http://article.nationalreview.com/?q=YjdjY2Y2YWU5YjQ1Y2Y5Mzg0MGRl NDQ4YTkwYmI2ZDE=

13. Ibid.

14. McCarthy, Andrew C. "Why Won't Obama Talk About Columbia?" *NRO.* 7 October 2008. http://article.nationalreview.com/?q=NjY4YzdhMDBkZGQ3ZmU2MTUzYjd kMzc5ZjUzYmViZWM=

Chapter 15: The Obamanutz Cult

1. "Poll: Obama More Popular than Jesus, Gandhi and Martin Luther King, Jr." *Foxnews.com.* 21 February 2009. http://www.foxnews.com/politics/first100days/2009/02/21/poll-obama-popular-jesus-gandhi-king/

2. Wallace-Wells, Ben. "Destiny's Child: No Candidate Since Robert F Kennedy Has Sparked as Much Campaign Trail Heat as Barack Obama. But Can the One-Term Senator Craft a Platform to Match His Charisma?" *Rolling Stone.* 22 February 2007. http://www.rollingstone.com/politics/story/13390609/campaign_08_the_radical_roots_of_barack_obama/3

3. Ibid.

4. Skenazy, Lenore. "The Obama Cult" Not for Everyone." *The New York Sun.* 20 February 2008. http://www.nysun.com/new-york/obama-cult-not-for-everyone/71569/.

5. Goldberg, Bernard. *A Slobbering Love Affair: The True (and Pathetic) Story of the Torrid Romance Between Barack Obama and the Mainstream Media.* Washington, DC: Regnery Publishing, Inc, 2009.

6. Skenazy, Lenore. "The Obama Cult" Not for Everyone." *The New York Sun.* 20 February 2008. http://www.nysun.com/new-york/obama-cult-not-for-everyone/71569/.

7. Beran, Michael Knox. "Obama, Shaman." *City Journal.* Summer 2008; Vol. 18, No. 3. http://www.city-journal.org/2008/18_3_obama.html

8. Ibid.

9. Ibid.

10. Goldberg, Bernard. *A Slobbering Love Affair: The True (and Pathetic) Story of the Torrid Romance Between Barack Obama and the Mainstream Media.* Washington, DC: Regnery Publishing, Inc, 2009.

11. Ibid, Pg. 18

12. Ibid, pg. 6.

13. Freddoso, David. *The Case Against Barack Obama: The Unlikely Rise and Unexamined Agenda of the Media's Favorite Candidate.* Washington, DC: Regnery, 2008, Pg. 63.

14. Nichanian, Daniel. "Cult-Like Chant Does Not Translate into Real Change." *Yale Daily News.* 18 February 2008. http://www.yaledailynews.com/articles/view/23595

15. Ibid.

16. Grey, Alan. "Pledge of Allegiance Becomes Pledge to Obama." *Newsblaze.* 27 January 2009. http://newsblaze.com/story/20090127224509nnnn.nb/topstory.html.

17. Bosch, Adam. "Police Bust Sullivan Ring Dealing 'Obama' Heroin." *Recordonline.* 23 January 2009. http://www.recordonline.com/apps/pbcs.dll/article?AID=/20090123/NEWS/901230343

18. Ruggeri, Amanda. "Chia Obama? Welcome to the Selling of a President." *US News & World Report.* 12 February 2009. http://www.usnews.com/articles/news/obama/2009/02/12/chia-obama-welcome-to-the-selling-of-a-president.html

19. Carnes, Patrick J PhD. *The Betrayal Bond: Breaking Free of Exploitive Relationships.* Deerfield Beach, FL: Health Communications, Inc, 1997.

20. Glick, Caroline B. "Obama the Savior". *Jewish World Review.* 22 April 2008. http://www.jewishworldreview.com/0408/glick042208.php3

21. Millegan, Robert. "Audit: Open Your Eyes KGB Officer Explains Russian NOW Agenda for 'Amerika'." *Cia-drugs.* 5 June 2009. http://www.mail-archive.com/cia-drugs@yahoogroups.com/msg12782.html

Index

About the Author

Joy Tiz, Joytiz.com, born in Chicago, recalls when many democrats were actually normal people who were just wrong about everything. Joy holds a M.Sc. in psychology and a JD in law.

Joy, a columnist for *Canada Free Press* wrote for *America's Voices* and has written extensively on topics including the legal aspects of self defense, canine behavior and politics. Her book *I Love My Dog, But . . .* (Avon 1999) received excellent reviews.

An unapologetic capitalist, Joy currently owns a real estate brokerage. She is also the owner of three magnificent and staunchly conservative German Shepherds, a Quarter Horse lacking in work ethic and Zirc the Wonder Colt.

Made in the USA
Lexington, KY
25 November 2009